ADVANCE PRA
FOCUSING ON TH‗ ‗‗
BY TERRY POWER

"An inspiring and important work on that invisible quality that shapes and defines the success or failure of organisations - its Service culture. This should be required reading for anyone interested in taking their business to the next level and doing so with integrity and good will."

- Keith Mogford.
Regional Manager of The Apprentice and Training Company

"Essential reading for anyone serious about mastering customer service. Terry's use of everyday events and experiences to emphasise the key messages is unique and effective."

- Steve Mitchinson
Customer Relationships Manager, B-Digital

"Terry has written a very good book. Read it. He will give you the key to attracting business in a manner far more powerful than any ad could hope for. When people feel important, they love to give you business. Terry will show you how it's done. And what's more, he'll give it to you in simple language."

- Glenn Cardwell.
Author, Consultant and speaker

1

"Terry Power is a master at relationships. If you need to know how to increase the connection with your customers and your staff, then this book is for you."

- Tracey McGrath
Conflict specialist and psychologist

"Terry Power rightly reminds us that whatever business we are in, our business IS service - and that the quality of our service will determine the quality of our results. His message - that service is based on the quality of our interactions with customers and clients - deserves to be heard. Those who heed his call will prosper in the new business environment because they will be giving their clients and customers exactly what they really want. This well-written and practical book should be mandatory reading for everyone in business. If it were widely read and acted upon, it sure would improve things for us all."

- Steve Wells
Psychologist, professional speaker and author

"Terry's message is simple, powerful and very visible. Focusing on the Invisible will become a basic tool for people around the world who want to achieve Service Excellence within their networks of clients, communities and peers. His message is definitely a global message."

- Robyn Henderson
Author, speaker and Global Networking Specialist

"In 'Focusing on the Invisible' Terry Power is able to create messages of wisdom through his business expertise, his diverse background and the eyes and stories of his children. In doing so he creates simple, effective and powerful messages for us all about the nature and importance of creating cultures of Service Excellence. Read, enjoy and prosper."

- Glenn Capelli
Churchill Fellow, author and speaker

"Terry presents highly important and highly relevant ideas in a simple, readable way. I recommend it to anybody interested in gaining an edge for their organisation through excellent customer Service."

- Gihan Perera
Internet consultant, First Step

"This is the first book I have read on the subject of business and customer satisfaction that made sense to me, and was speaking to me directly. I think Terry is on to something here, and it isn't invisible when you see the results on the faces of those who experience it. Although he does focus on the issues of customer satisfaction and Service at all times in a highly practical way, he is really describing how he manages to deliver his inner feeling state to the situation. And it produces results! This is the reason we like to go to certain shops or organisations or people for our requirements: to share in that feeling."

- Dr Dave Lake.
Author, consultant and medical doctor

FOCUSING ON THE INVISIBLE

Terry Power

First published in 2001
Comet Publishing, Perth, Western Australia
Fax: 61 8 9537 3889
Email: comet@execedge.com.au
URL: www.execedge.com.au

National Library of Australia
Cataloguing-in-Publication entry:

Power, Terry, 1961-.
Focusing on the Invisible:
Creating a Culture of Service Excellence

ISBN 0 957439 0 3.

Customer Service. I. Title.

658 .812

Cover Design by Shaan Coutinho,
Watermark Graphic Design

DEDICATION

This book is dedicated to my Mum.
You may be invisible now Mum, but you
are forever in my heart.

CONTENTS

Acknowledgments

A book, like many things in life, is largely created from the invisible. As the reader, you only see the printed word upon the paper. Behind those words are not only many hours of labour but also many, many wonderful people who made it possible.

Stories are not created from thin air. They are inspired by careful observation of the important experiences that happen around and to you. In my life there are no more important experiences than those I have with my family. To my children, Cameron, Monique, Dennis, Stevie and Cassie thank you for enriching my life far beyond any father's wishes. I love you all deeply.

To my Mum and Dad, thank you for being the greatest parents that ever lived. If my family love me even half as much as I love you, I will die a happy man.

To Steve Wells, you have been my mentor my colleague and above all my friend. Thanks for believing in me, especially in those times when I didn't.

To my editor, Chris Kenworthy, whose patience and ability to see clearly what needs to be done is second to none.

To my many colleagues, clients and friends. There are too many of you to name individually, but my thanks go out to you just the same. It would be an injustice, however, to neglect to mention some of you by name. To David Lake for encouraging me to show him my work, if not for you it could well have remained forever invisible. To Tracey McGrath, a friend whom I have both cried and laughed with. To Noel Fossilo, a client I now call, "Mate". To Steve Mitchinson, who really understands the true meaning of the word Service. To Glenn Capelli, a mentor and a goal to aspire to from afar. To Robyn Henderson, who knows the importance of the invisible in networking. To Gihan Perera, for his quiet and persistent encouragement.

Lastly, and most importantly, I thank the most beautiful, caring woman I have ever had the pleasure to Serve. My wife, Heather. My love, you have always been there for me, you are my true inspiration, my support, my life. Without you, the world may as well be invisible, for it would hardly be worth living. I love you always.

WHAT IS SUCCESS?

To laugh often and much;

To win the respect of intelligent people
and the affection of children;

To earn the appreciation of honest critics
and endure the betrayal of false friends;

To appreciate beauty;

To find the best in others;

To leave the world a bit better, whether
by a healthy child, a garden patch or
a redeemed social condition;

To know that even one life has breathed
easier because you have lived;

This is to have succeeded.

Ralph Waldo Emerson

Introduction

I once read a quote that said, 'In five years from now you will be the same person you are today, except for the people you meet, the books you read and the information you listen to.' It could be true. But I don't think so.

Many of the people that continue to inspire, motivate and give me ideas have been around a lot longer than five years. My wife, Heather, is certainly my greatest inspiration and support. Another person who has influenced my life, probably more than he realises, is my brother, Alan. In some ways, the whole message of this book can be traced back to something he once said to me.

Alan is a psychologist. This means that, ordinarily, I don't take any notice of his philosophising. Fortunately, this time I did.

One day while I was deep in study he took me aside.

'Terry,' he said. 'For years you've been studying all this stuff about human learning and interaction.'

'Yeah,' I replied

'Well, there is really only one thing you need to know about us human beings, and when you know this one thing, every interaction you ever have will take on a new meaning.'

He was starting to get my attention.

'Well, what is it?' I asked nonchalantly, trying to feign disinterest.

'Every person you meet has around their neck an invisible sign.'

I felt my attention and interest slip a few notches. I imagined that he was going to wander off into another of his psychobabble talks.

'Oh, really.'

'I'm not kidding,' he enthused. 'It's true. And once you know what is written on that sign, it will change your life forever.'

'Okay, Al. You've got me.'

Make me feel important. Those four words have changed my life forever.

'Upon the chest of every person, there is a sign with these words emblazoned: Make me feel important.' Those four words have changed my life forever.

Since that conversation, I have dedicated my life focusing on those invisible words and what they can mean in creating cultural change. Remembering them has always served me well. I have had the pleasure of working with people from many walks of life: CEO's, office clerks, construction workers, politicians, directors, criminals, children and customers (and many that fit into more than one category). These people are all clearly different, but in my experience, one thing unites them. They all want to feel important.

A Culture of Service Excellence certainly sounds grandiose, but what exactly does it mean?

Ordinarily I don't condone violence. But to give this sentence meaning let's begin by tearing it apart. There are three key words in this statement: Culture, Service and Excellence. Each reveals some truths in relation to

16

the context of this book. Let's briefly examine them.

Culture is an elusive, albeit an ever-present, creature. It is something we interact with continuously. But when we try to pin it down it slips easily through our intellectual grasp. Culture, like air through a moving hand we can't capture it, but we all know it's there. And vital for our survival. Despite its pervasiveness it remains invisible. In its totality it makes up the inherited ideas, beliefs, values and knowledge

> *Service touches lives and is integral to what it means to be a human being.*

which constitute the *shared* vision of any nation, group or, in the context of this book, any organisation. Something so important requires us to investigate its implications within our organisations.

Service, too, has in the past been narrowly defined. Basically, service is helping or assisting others. In reality it cuts much deeper than that. In its purest form Service touches lives and is integral to what it means to be a human being. My definition of Service is inspired by the work of Robert K Greenleaf. Greenleaf created a form of leadership based on Service – Servant Leadership. In his words, "Servant Leadership encourages collaboration, trust, foresight, listening, and the ethical use of power and empowerment.

"The servant-leader is servant first…It begins with the natural feeling that one wants to serve, to serve first…The best test, and most difficult to administer, is: do those served grow as persons; do they, while being served, become healthier, wiser, freer, more autonomous". I believe that the Service I am advocating meets this test. This is Service with a captial 'S'.

Which only leaves us with the last key word; Excellence. Excellent Service is more than enriching people's lives. It is about continually, endlessly and passionately seeking ways to do it better.

It is about continually, endlessly and passionately seeking ways to do it better.

This book is dedicated to creating a culture that makes yourself, others and your customers feel important. This is the foundation on which a Culture of Service Excellence is built.

Terry Power
November 2001

CHAPTER ONE

Focusing on the Invisible:
Creating a Culture of Service Excellence

Things I couldn't see have always fascinated me. I remember sitting outside the girls' changing rooms at school. I'd sit, longingly daydreaming about the terrific advantage I'd have if only I could see what all my mates couldn't.

Some things, it would seem, never change. Ever since leaving school all I've ever wanted in anything I did was an unfair advantage. It's taken two decades of business, three university degrees and more failures than I care to remember, but I think I've finally got a clue as to where that advantage is hidden. Maybe I just learn slower than others.

> *Ever since leaving school all I've ever wanted in anything I did was an unfair advantage.*

And the great revelation?

The key to business success comes in two parts.

One, how we *Serve* our customers.

And two, the internal organisational *Culture* that drives that service.

Okay, it's not rocket science. It's not even really a revelation. But it is still critically important. Given that, why does it seem so many organisations stuff it up?

I reckon it's because many of the things needed to build a Culture which satisfies, delights and makes

19

customers feel good are *nigh on* invisible. So, it's easy to forget them.

Now I don't mean invisible like mysterious poltergeists, ghosts or things that go bump in the night. Although that can satisfy some customers, depending on what line of work you're in. I mean those things that seem *so small* as to be almost invisible. The unseen attention to detail, those little common courtesies and the unspoken thoughts, about 'how we do business around here'. Important? Yes. But easily forgotten. It is in those all-too-rare moments when these intangibles are present that customers feel special and important. My brother was right. People do want you to make them feel important. In my experience, when people feel important, they also feel good – whatever that means to them.

When you boil down all the hype and all the pompous theorising, that's all Service is really. Making people feel good.

In the final analysis, Service is about making people *feel* good.

I don't mean roll-over-and-fall-down-drunk good, I mean feeling good about themselves and feeling good about doing business with you. When you boil down all the hype and all the pompous theorising, that's all Service is really. Making people feel good. Good about themselves, good about being a customer, and good about doing business with you.

Don't get me wrong. I understand that there is a lot more to this than a dopey smile and a warm handshake. But don't discount the power of making your customers feel good. There are lots of things that make people feel good. When they have received excellent value for money. When a competent and caring assistant has served them well. When the product has surpassed their wildest expectations (don't laugh, it does happen). These and a raft of other big and little things make customers feel good.

But Wait, There's More

Sure, you want your customer to walk away feeling good. If they do, you know they'll tell others. But there is another pleasantly unsuspected by-product of excellent Service. The customer isn't the only one to benefit, because everyone feels good.

Not like a New-Years-party kind of feel-good. More like an *I'm-part-of-something-that-matters-here* feeling. Think about it. Last time you were a customer that came away from a Service happy with the outcome, didn't you get a sense that the person who served you also felt good? A sense that the person felt they too were doing something important? Or perhaps you can remember the last time you did something exceptional (some people may have to delve deeper into their past than others).

What about the last time you made a customer laugh? Didn't you enjoy the fun also? Did your work feel more meaningful after assisting a customer through a problem, or teaching them something new or showing them how to get the most from your Service?

In a good Service transaction, *everyone* feels good, and *everyone* benefits. Isn't that a worthwhile goal in itself? Every time human beings come in contact with

21

each other there exists an opportunity for both to be richer for the experience. For a little magic to occur.

I'm not trying to be all misty-eyed and mushy here. The hard fact is that people who provide excellent Service pull rabbits out of hats; rabbits that are the right size, just the right colour and bounce at just the right height. And the final result? Everyone feels pretty darn good about it.

People who provide excellent Service pull rabbits out of hats; rabbits that are the right size, just the right colour and bounce at just the right height.

Those of us that deal with customers – and we all do in one form or another – have the opportunity to experience these moments of magic every day. For it is during all those fleeting moments, those seemingly insignificant interactions, that a Culture of excellent Service is created.

If you want a techo book, this ain't it

This book isn't about your products or your technical knowledge. Other industry-specific books deal with that, and I highly recommend that you get your hands on them. You might like to read them too. Right now, we are concerned with more important stuff. Its no good building a better mouse-trap (the product) if every time you show it to your customer (the Service) the trap ends up dangling from the pointy end of their nose (the disaster).

This book has a bunch of ideas for creating more fulfilling Service, and a Culture of excellence, with a lesson or three thrown in. But you will also find a recurrent theme: If any organisation is to elevate Service to its fullest potential then *everyone* **in the organisation must focus on aligning the attitudes, the values and the beliefs with making the customer feel important**.

This is vital.

Not withstanding the fact that your product/Service must fill a customer need, and do it well, the way it is delivered is a key issue in the world of Service.

What is this animal called Service?

There has been much written about the definition of Service. Particularly good Service. Seems to me everyone talks about it; few understand it. All organisations want it; few obtain it. Ask 500 delegates in a seminar, and you could get 500 different answers. You may hear; 'Listening to the client', 'Satisfying the customer's needs', 'Delighting the client'. All could be right.

However, I think it is even simpler than this. In its simplest form, I believe good Service is a transfer of feeling. A feeling that all expectations have been met or surpassed. The customer is happy with the Service and the provider is happy doing the serving. For this to happen you need a Culture of Service Excellence.

The pickle-faced shop assistant

If you doubt this, just remember the last time you walked into a shop and were met by a disgruntled, grumpy, downright-miserable shop assistant. You know the type.

23

Like they'd had a bowl of pickles for breakfast and for the rest of the morning they'd been sucking on lemons, all swilled down with a glass or two of vinegar. Ugh!

One look tells you they wish they'd never got up this morning. After a second look, you're wishing they hadn't. Did that feeling come across? Sure it did. I doubt very much you went away clicking your heels and singing, 'I'm on top of the world, looking down on creation'. Fact is, one encounter like that goes a long way toward ruining your whole day.

In its simplest form, I believe good Service is a transfer of feeling.

On the other hand, recall the last time you rang a number for assistance and were greeted by a happy, competent operator who treated you like the very important person that you are. A person that went out of their way to fulfil your needs. A person who cared about you and your feelings.

'Good morning, Mr Power,' they chirped. 'How might I be of assistance to you today?' Then they set about making sure that they were of assistance. These rare individuals can turn you around even when your mood is similar to that of the 'pickle-faced' shop assistant. How did you start to feel then? At a subconscious level, you know they treated you importantly. You can't fake that. You can't see it, you can't fake it. Could it be that somewhere deep in your subconscious you were thinking, 'Wow. That person really cared about me'. I believe that is exactly what you did. I have experienced both sides of this Service coin. I bet you have too. At the end of the day, I know which company will get my future business. I bet I know which will get yours, too.

The era of the Pokemon.

There was a time when if you had a product that everybody wanted, but nobody had, and you could deliver, you had it made. Not any more.

Now, the moment you make it, and before you can say Pokemon, the Japanese have built it smaller, faster and with more gadgets than you can poke a remote control at. At the risk of sounding hackneyed, it's not what you do but the way that you do it. This book is founded on the simple premise that: **if while doing business you make the customer feel important, they'll spend more, you get greater customer loyalty, a happier work force and increased productivity.**

For this to happen you must create, nurture and maintain the right Culture.

Emotions and decisions

Emotions provide the electrical current for driving our motions. E-motions, if you like.

I am suggesting the key factors in any Service transaction are the feelings of the Service provider and the customer. First in the equation are the feelings of the Service provider. How she felt about herself, her company and the value of her work. Secondly, the customer. How he felt he was being treated. How competently he felt the provider did her job. How important she made him feel. All these feelings affect on the perceived level of Service. Note that there is no objective measurement in place here. No benchmark. No scale by which to judge. Just plain, simple, subjective feelings.

25

Transferring feelings

Make no mistake; feelings are a key element in any Service transaction. It seems to me that banks have lost sight of this simple truth. There is not a great deal of positive feeling transferred from the smiling digital face of an ATM computer screen.

Emotions provide the electrical current for driving our motions. E-motions, if you like.

It is worth noting that feelings transfer rapidly. **They transfer swiftly, silently and as assuredly as bank fees from your savings account. The difference is you have control over the feelings you part with.** Unfortunately, the same can't be said about the way they transfer their fees from us to them.

Transferring positive feelings that boldly, yet invisibly, state, 'I am happy to be of Service to you, whilst you are here, I will give you my full attention,'should reside at the core of all excellent Service.

So, if the transfer is to be a positive one, the person providing the Service will be feeling pretty good about themselves also.

In a world of change, one of the casualties is this notion of quality Service. It is becoming a rare and endangered species.

Good Service ... or what remains of this animal, is becoming a rare species.

Excellent Service is a contagious feeling.

Action Steps

- Always remember that whatever you are thinking, it's on show. Whatever your staff think and feel is on full display. Thoughts and feelings may seem invisible, but you might as well be wearing a neon sign boldly flashing every thought and emotion. When you feel something, your colleagues know and the customer knows.

- **Begin each day knowing that you have a choice. The choice to give exceptional Service.** The choice to make something special happen. As human beings, choice is our greatest power. Exercise it every day.

In a world of change, one of the casualties is this notion of quality Service. It is becoming a rare and endangered species.

- Start to notice and see the invisible. Listen, look and sense the feelings and beliefs of others as they go about their business of serving customers.

We ignore the little things at our peril

If you neglect those little things, the only time you might see your customers come back is with a baseball bat in hand! I'm not joking. I once worked with a team of vehicle examiners. For some little reason or another, one of their customers was upset. And he let them know. After having a work order put on his car, he got out, walked around to the back of the car, pulled out a block-splitter (a five kilo hammer-type axe) and proceeded to smash his car to pieces. That's feedback. If we fail to read the feedback, chances are we'll fail. And there is no excuse because feedback is everywhere. Right down to the smallest of smallest things. Even in your DNA.

What is your DNA showing?

The human body is a remarkable thing. More complex than anything known to humanity. Amazingly, every detail is contained in microscopic DNA encoded in every cell. We now know that we can take any cell of the body and learn every other characteristic of the organism. This incredible phenomenon has its parallel in the material world. In the hologram, for example. If you were able to take a holographic image and smash it on to the floor, you would see some interesting stuff. The first thing you would notice is that you are no longer looking at a broken piece. Rather, you would see a complete copy of the entire image. This is unlike a normal image. If, for example you were looking at an image of a flower and it broke you would notice several things. There would be a petal on one piece, a stem on another and so on. However, with a broken holographic image you would see lots of little but complete flowers. Each piece represents the whole.

He got out, walked around to the back of the car, pulled out a block-splitter (a five kilo hammer-type axe) and proceeded to smash his car to pieces. That's feedback.

I think there is a parallel here with Service organisations. At least in the mind of the client.

The way a customer is treated by the Service desk, on the telephone or in the lobby is exposing the blueprint of the whole company. When the customer interacts with that one individual, it is as if they were looking at the very DNA of the organisation. If the Service is exceptional, then the organisation is exceptional. If the Service is poor then the organisation is also rotten.

Action Steps

- Understand that every interaction with the customer is impact-full. Every interaction represents the whole. Each person within your organisation is like a strand of DNA representative of the whole Culture. **Let the strands in your DNA be positive.**

Individuals not groups

Individuals buy from individuals, not from corporations. In the final analysis, you are only ever dealing with individuals. It matters not that the person represents a multimillion-dollar multinational company. The customer you must be concerned with is the one sitting opposite you right now. Tom Peters talks about the 'belly to belly' relationship. I'm not sure I want to be that intimate, but you get the picture. All the statistics and personality-typing in the world is useless if the person in front of you defies categorisation. And most do. Sure they lean towards one way or the other, but ultimately human beings are incredibly complex. That wonderful thinker Glenn Capelli puts it this way, 'We should label jars not people'. Honour the way the person is right now and reject the idea of labelling the person an X type, Y type person, hows-your-father-type. Applying formulae to humans is not only misleading; it can sometimes be damaging. Just as every fingerprint in the world is a complex, infinitely different shape, so too are the personalities of everyone you meet. When you put people in boxes you run the risk of seeing people only in that light. It is worth studying human behaviour to see what preferences people might have, but use it only as a guide.

Understand that every interaction with the customer is impact-full. Every interaction represents the whole.

Action Steps

- Always remember you are only ever dealing with individuals. Not herds of lemmings.

- Beware of personality typing; it pigeonholes people and people are not pigeons.

CHAPTER TWO

The Secret of Service

In the eye of the storm

For most people the world is not what it used to be. Of course not. Many a poet has observed that nothing endures but change. Right now, change is cranking up at an alarming pace, and from every direction. Think about it. The population is increasing, technology is multiplying and doubling its power at a break-neck pace, and Service is slipping into the doldrums. That's how I see things as a customer. All the research I have seen in this area supports my view. A whole raft of studies confirm that the gap is widening between the customer's expectation of Service and the actual Service delivered. The gap has widened to a chasm. Summaries of this information conclude that up to 82% of customers chose not to do repeat business with the same company because of 'attitudes of indifferent customer Service'.

Applying formulae to humans is not only misleading; it can sometimes be damaging.

Despite this malaise, all too many management teams mosey along oblivious to the madness whipping around them. Like being in the eye of a storm, they sit contented in the calm of their office, wondering what all the fuss is about. If only they were to step outside, reality would drag them into the spinning madness around them. But unless we stop to think, it is easy to believe that we are

31

sitting safely outside it all. This couldn't be further from the truth.

Recently I read a story about a tornado that struck a small town in America. Ripping up trees and flipping cars, it caused extensive damage. After it had blown over, the townspeople came out from under their tables and into the streets to survey the damage. They thought they were safe. Then it struck them. The other side of the storm came crashing through, this time taking lives as well as trees and cars. At the moment of quiet, the townspeople had been in the eye of the storm.

So it is for many managers. Blissfully unaware, they sit in the security of their offices, thumbing aimlessly through reports. Sooner or later, the storm is going to move over. Unprepared, they will be thrust into the turmoil until they are dumped back to the ground, left only to pick up the broken pieces. It's time for these managers to wake up and stick their head out. The best way to manage has always been and always will be by getting out there amongst the workers. Before the storm hits. It is in the fields of battle that leaders get a feel for what the people are thinking and by extension what their customers are thinking.

The impact of change on Service

The impact of significant change is affecting our daily lives more now than ever before. Our neighbours come and go and we don't even learn their names (except maybe in the civil law courts. 'Well, their fence was over my side.') The 'personalised' singing Christmas card we get has more computing power than the first rocket shot into the sub-zero temperatures of icy space – and is about as warm. And 'customer care' is a hackneyed phrase, not a way of doing business.

Simply put. Service, *just isn't!*

When the Australia Customer Service Association commissioned a report on Service recovery, they discovered some interesting findings. The brief of the study was to review the 'complaints Culture' within Australia. It is worth noting that the summary indicated that effective complaints handling is an effective way of building customer loyalty. It provides an avenue to market research of customers' opinions, and gives an organisation a last ditch attempt to turn the customer around.

Despite these findings, in Australia the culture of our organisations just does not make it easy for people to complain.

Like being in the eye of a storm, they sit contented in the calm of their office, wondering what all the fuss is about.

Working with many organisations has provided me with much anecdotal evidence to suggest that Service expectations are growing significantly in this country. Yet people are still not complaining. Other studies add weight to this anecdotal evidence, and cite reasons why this is so.

Another study commissioned by the Service Institute of Australia indicated that there are two major reasons why people don't complain - lack of time (61%) and too much trouble (55%).

There is, then, an urgent need to develop systems that make it easier for customers to complain. If the complaint is not heard, then the customer is likely to take their business elsewhere and an opportunity to win back a customer, and possibly even an advocate, has been lost.

It would seem that people have got so used to poor Service they don't even bother complaining. At least not to the organisation. But, make no mistake, they will tell as many other people as care to listen. And plenty do.

Many companies pay lip service to customer care and Service, but how many give meaningful, practical training that shifts that invisible quality – attitude – towards extraordinary Service?

The best way to manage has always been and always will be by getting out there amongst the workers.

A lot of training skirts around the issue of attitude, but focuses more on techniques and other tricks to sell customers. People do not want to be sold; they want to be wooed.

Think of a time when someone really gave you exceptional Service. What did they do? Chances are they showed genuine care and concern for your needs. That's not selling, that's wooing.

Positive attitude is fundamental to Service – make it a priority.

Start where you are – and know which way you are heading

In that classic tale Alice in Wonderland, the Cheshire Cat says to Alice, 'If you don't know where you are going any road will get you there.' How true. And I would add, 'If you don't know where you are now, you'll never get there anyway'. Simply stated, you must know where you are starting from. This is true of a chosen destination, a distant goal and your level of Service. If you don't take stock, how are you going to know which way is up? Which way is progress? Or what is the best thing for you to do right now? Without this information, you could be streaking ahead…in the wrong direction. Blasting along westward on an Australian highway hoping to catch a sunrise is a very foolish thing to do. It's no use scorching ahead in a streamlined and efficient manner if you're heading the wrong way. Obvious, right? You would think so. But this is another of those simple things that is perhaps so simple it gets forgotten. The importance of knowing where 'here' is, was driven home to me many years ago…

A traveller's experience

In my younger days (actually the days weren't any younger but there were certainly less wrinkles in them) I did a lot of travelling. On one of my more extended journeys, I found myself in a small country town. You know the ones. A main street, a pub, a Centrelink and another pub, a TAB and, oh yes, another pub. As I rode in (on a motorcycle, not a horse) I looked around for something that remotely resembled life. Country towns are like that. Deserted. After riding around for awhile and not seeing so much as a friendly ATM, I had almost given up hope. Lucky for me they had one of those wonderful 'tourist bays' with the big – albeit dilapidated - signs showing the local town site. I checked out the board. Sure enough, it showed the whereabouts of the town shearing shed, the museum for modern crutching machines and other fascinating artefacts. These were, as it turned out, the town 'highlights'. All well and good. But the *You are here* sign had either fallen off, or was never there in the first place. I drove around that town for ages trying to find out where here

People do not want to be sold; they want to be wooed.

was. If I was to get anywhere in that town, I had to first know my current position. It is the same in Service. When you look around your organisation, you may well have a clear idea of the whereabouts of the sheep dippers and the people most likely to do the crutching, but do you know where you are positioned in your customer's mind?

Your positioning

When a customer is thinking of your Service, how do they rank you? Are they thinking, 'Yeah, they make the best crutching machines,' or, 'Crikey, that mob. They make the worst crutching machines.' Or, worse still, 'Well blow me down, I didn't even know that they made crutching machines.'

Positioning in the customer's mind must be done in steps. Firstly, you want to know what message is already out there. This is your *You are here.* Secondly, you want to know where to direct those customers. These are your highlights. Begin within your organisational walls, with your people. But you have to be honest. If you are number two, three or four, say so, as long as you frame it in a way that lets people know you are not stuck there. People appreciate knowing where they are. I know I do. They appreciate honesty, too.

Action Steps

- Begin now to take stock of where you are positioned in the market place, in your organisation and in your best customer's minds.

- Create a map with clear reference points on it so people can see where they are now and where you want to take them.

Service is not some thing you do

After presenting a seminar, I got speaking to some of the delegates. One delegate was a real estate agent who worked in my local area. I recognised her immediately. It seemed like her picture was on every second house in the district. Not on wanted posters, on the real estate signs. It turned out she had been 'working' the area about 18 months, and in that time she had practically cornered the market. In speaking with her I soon realised she had a clear understanding of Service. She told me that everyone was a potential customer and so every interaction for her was a Service transaction. She clearly understood that Service is not something you switch on and off like a water valve. It is everywhere – a Culture. The customer flow is constant.

Blasting along westward on an Australian highway hoping to catch a sunrise is a very foolish thing to do.

She understood that every time someone interacts with a customer, they are providing Service. What's more, in the mind of the customer, they represent the company. They speak on behalf of the company, so they are the company. You can't switch Service on and off like a machine. For a company to be successful, they have to live it. This philosophy reaps benefits. This real estate woman understood this too.

She clearly understood that Service is not something you switch on and off like a water valve.

Judging by the number of 'SOLD' stickers, under all her pictures, she is very successful. When you talk to her you cannot help but notice how she lives and breathes Service. The words emblazoned on all of her marketing material sum it up: *'Real estate is not my business, it's my life'*.

Now, I am not suggesting that your work is everything. I think that balance is extremely important in any life. What I am saying is that while you are at work, Service had better be...everything. It is foolhardy to section off Service as a specialist area – to be cranked up only when there is a perceived need. For any organisation to thrive everyone needs to be mindful of the importance of the customer. At all times. With apologies to the management guru, Peter Drucker – 'the only reason for business to exist is to creatively serve the customer'.

Service orientation is not something you do it is something you must be.

Action Steps

- Brief everyone in your organisation on the importance of comprehensive customer care. At all times.

- Remind people that everyone is a potential customer – internal or external.

- If the premise is correct that 'at all times we are selling something', then it follows that someone is always being a customer. Ask yourself the question, If I were a customer right now, how would I like to be treated? That may not be exactly how the person in front of you wants to be treated, but it's a fair starting point.

Beware of the measurement trap

If you can't measure it, you can't manage it. This is a common belief amongst management consultants. I think they're wrong. They are wrong because it is exactly the things you cannot measure that are often the most important. I know my children love me (especially on pocket money day), but I challenge you to measure that. In a previous life as a manager, I knew I had the respect of my employees. I never thought it possible or desirable to quantify their level of loyalty. I've had many businesses, but never found an accurate way to measure my customers' satisfaction. I have seen countless psychological and management tests designed to

> *Do what you do so well that people cannot help but talk positively about you.*

measure everything from customers' attitude to customers' anxiety. All with about as much accuracy as predicting the astrological stars of my pet guinea pig. (I think she is an Aries – she's very jumpy).

It seems to me that **the only real test of a customer's satisfaction is whether they would either refer, or do business with you again**.

This is not to suggest that we shouldn't measure aspects of our business. Clearly, we should. But when it comes to customer satisfaction, there should be no margin for error. No matter what organisation I ran or consulted with, my goal has always been the same. To build a Culture that demands Service Excellence. My objective is always to stack up so many little things alongside the big things, that the customer can't help but love doing business with us. The aim is simply this: Do what you do so well that people cannot help but talk positively about you.

Customer Service surveys

As a consultant I am often asked, 'Should we do a survey to measure customer satisfaction?'

To which I reply, 'Have you ever heard the quote about statistics? ...Well, it should have read 'Lies, damn lies and surveys'.' Like a government report at election time, surveys can say anything the creator wants them to. And if the creator doesn't have a clue what she wants it to say – well the survey can say that too!

Study after study has shown that customer Service surveys are a very inaccurate tool when it comes to the measurement of customer satisfaction and loyalty. One

Harvard Business Reviewer put it this way: 'As tools for the value a company delivers to its customers, satisfaction surveys are imperfect. As tools for predicting whether customers will purchase more of the company's products and Services, they are *grossly imperfect*'.

Like a government report at election time, surveys can say anything the creator wants them to.

The fact is, surveys do not give a clear picture of the satisfaction they purport to measure. Why? Because people don't believe they are going to be listened to anyway. So they do what any rational thinking human being would do when faced with filling in a form. They lie.

Better to ask

The best way I have found to measure customer satisfaction is to ask. Not in a survey. They are boring to take and boring to give. What's more, surveys only discover what a customer *thinks* you want to know. There is a better way. The follow-up 'courtesy call'. Using a form and a formula, this type of feedback mechanism can give great insights into customer satisfaction. Here's an example of what I am talking about:

'Hi, Monique here from Power Presentations just making a courtesy call to thank you for doing business with us, as well as to get a feel for how satisfied you are with the last presentation we gave at your organisation. Do you have a moment right now?'

Ask a few prompting, open-ended questions, then sit back, and listen. You'd be amazed at what people will tell you once you get chatting with them.

No matter what they tell you, always close by thanking them. After all, you want their present and future business, or at least you want them referring business to you.

Action Steps

- Review the way you get feedback from your customers. Are you sending out great wads of paperwork for people to fill out? Are you getting, at best, dubious results and at worst, no results?

- Make it easy for customers to give you feedback. Look for any legitimate opportunity to contact your customers directly and solicit their feelings.

- Always acknowledge your customers, no matter what feedback they give you. Feedback is valuable. Treat it as such.

- Once you have collated what your customers are saying, act on it. As soon as possible.

CHAPTER THREE

The Personal Touch

Customer Service: the greatest modern myth

Stop and ask one hundred people in the street their thoughts on today's customer Service and you would find that ninety-five of them think the statement is an oxymoron. (An oxymoron is a contradiction in terms, not, as I first thought an idiot that works in a diver's tanks factory). Truth is, customers no longer feel as if they are getting real Service. In the words of at least one respected researcher, 'We are experiencing a customer Service crisis… 'Crisis' is a strong word but no exaggeration. Most customer Service is poor, much of it is awful, and Service quality generally appears to be falling.'

> *Truth is, customers no longer feel as if they are getting real Service.*

There is good reason for this belief. We ring the 'customer Service' line only to be electronically told that our call is important. Please hold. For 25 minutes or more. We purchase something in a shop and while we once could expect a thank you, now we don't need it. Because, as I was once tersely told by a shop assistant, 'It's written on your docket'. We pull into the 'Service station' to be served. And get out in the rain to fill our car.

The days of the corner shop owner greeting you by

your name and inquiring as to the health of your mother and her ingrown toenail – as they are serving you with a slab of blue vein cheese – are well and truly long gone. No longer does the shop keeper/owner weigh your favourite lump of salami and spam and have it waiting for you on the customer counter. Now you are a number. A dollar figure. A commodity. An asset or a liability to be processed along with the cheese, the salami and the spam. And in many cases you are considered little more than a pain in the proverbial. A sort of, 'Business-and-service-would-be-a-fine-thing-if-it- weren't-for-the-customers,' kind of attitude.

Now you are a number. A dollar figure. A commodity. An asset or a liability to be processed along with the cheese, the salami and the spam.

Time for a change

Now I am not suggesting that we go back to this 'nostalgic' era in order to set our profits soaring. Certainly not. Many small businesses are going bankrupt because they refuse to change. Nor am I suggesting that being courteous alone is enough. If you teach an idiot to have manners, you just end up with a polite idiot. People who say please and thank you while they stuff-up your order are just plain irritating.

What I am saying is this: The first principle of Service is focusing on the person as a person not as a customer. A person with needs, wants and desires. Just like you. A person who wants to be satisfied in a way that makes them feel good. A person who wants to feel important. Just like you.

First and foremost, you are dealing with people. And people like to be treated as people, not as a plotting on a graph.

The first step in becoming more customer focused is to become more people focused.

Action Steps

- Treat every customer with care and caring. Always think of them as a person first and as a customer second.

- Catherine DeVrye says that one of the most important things to remember about customer relations is, 'Not to treat your customers like you treat your relations'. If you treat your relations badly, I agree with her.

Bricks, sand and mortification

More than two decades ago, at that hormone-challenging age of seventeen, I got my first taste of business. I wanted a job rubbing suntan lotion on the State netball team, but had to settle for working with my brother-in-law, who built brick letterboxes (you do what you can). I recall being amazed by how impressed people were with the little things he used to make me do.

After he built the letter box he would make me clear away all the rubble, throw a little clean, yellow sand around the base of the letter box and make sure that I was always *exceptionally* polite (a habit I had already inherited, no doubt, from my mother). It quickly became clear to me that people were 'sold' more on attitude than they were on any kind of exceptional ability to get the job done.

Looking back I realise he wasn't a great bricklayer. In fact, some of those letterboxes were, shall we say, a little bit iffy. I am convinced a similar letterbox built without those little extras would have left customers mortified. Getting the letter box built was important, but laying bricks is not that difficult – most people could do it if they took their time – what was more important was the way my brother-in-law insisted I dealt with the customer. My attitude.

I also learned something infinitely more important – a successful business is made up of dozens of little concrete things done exceptionally well.

I quickly reasoned that the little bit of sand made for good appearances, the clearing away of the debris made for ease of use, and the healthy dose of politeness smoothed the business transaction. These ideas and habits served me well later in business life. I also learned something infinitely more important – a successful business is made up of dozens of little concrete things done exceptionally well.

Indeed, the greatest reason customers are dissatisfied stems from personal interactions. A U.S. News and World report found that 82% of people leave because of a poor experience with the Service. If you're wondering about the other 18% these figures are made up of; better competition 9%, friendships 5%, change of location 3% and 1% because someone dies. You can't do much about the last category. I understand that. But it is possible to have a positive effect on the whopping 82%. This can make a big difference.

What makes the difference? In some cases its just a little shovelful of yellow sand. With a good measure of 'pleases' and 'thankyous' thrown in. Simple really, isn't it?

Lesson – don't try to measure customer satisfaction – do things that ensure it!

Action Steps

- Look at how much you are currently investing in surveys and then look at re-channelling it into non-formal approaches.

- Build in enough little things so that customers can't help but feel important. Continually look for small, unique ways to enhance the customer experience.

But they all look alike to me

During the last school term, one of my sons, Cameron, developed a business project as an assignment. Cameron decided he was going to sell pet bricks (his first idea was pet tigers, but I didn't have anywhere to cage them). When it came to pricing, he valued some of the bricks at $2.00 and some of the bricks at $3.00. I asked him what was the difference between the $2.00 brick and the $3.00 brick. His answer was simple and truthful - 'On the $3.00 brick I make an extra dollar'. Doesn't that have a parallel out there in the business world?

How often do we buy something because of its perceived value rather than its actual worth? Pre-loved clothing is a case in point. Clothes from charity recycling shops have a perceived lower value, but are they really worth any less? After all, they still cover your bits and keep you warm. As long as there are no holes where your bits usually are.

The challenge to you

The challenge in your business, whatever business that may be, is giving the customer a reason to buy your brick. Is yours better? Will it fill their need? Will the way they receive it make them feel important? The problem facing most businesses is that the bricks of their business and the bricks of all their competitors, are as similar as the ones stuck in a prison wall. And sometimes about as exciting.

They all look alike, they all smell alike and they all taste alike. (Yes, taste. Thousands of hours on a building site and you can *taste* the bricks). To the customer they just look like a bunch of bricks. So, they might as well buy the cheapest one. Unless you give them a reason to do otherwise. Here's an important question:

What's your point of difference?

It is a fact in the Service industry that most profitable strategies are built on differentiation. That means offering customers a real or perceived value that your competitors do not. Your company can differentiate itself at every point it comes in contact with your customers. This applies from the moment customers realise they need a Service (or even suspect they do) to the time when they dispose of it. And even beyond that. Organisations must broaden their thinking to encompass the customer's entire experience. There are a wealth of possibilities to uncover opportunities, to position your offerings in ways that neither you nor your competitors thought possible.

Back to the bricks

To me, all my son's bricks were much the same, the difference that he had created was only in perception. He said that he thought that they would be worth more because they had, 'more appeal'. I thought, 'Based on what criteria?' The same question applies to your point of difference. Ask yourself what you do, and how does that appeal to your customer? Do you offer a perceived point of difference? What is the perception you create in your customer's mind?

Organisations must broaden their thinking to encompass the customer's entire experience.

One real way of creating a unique view of your business is in the delivery of your Service. All things being equal, your Service offers the greatest point of leverage.

The closer your business matches your competitors the more crucial your Service becomes.

People need a reason to choose your organisation above the competitors; particularly if what you offer is more expensive. Your Service is the jewel that stands out in a sea of bricks. In essence, what you are trying to create is an impossible comparison between you and your competitors. Once you have established in the customer's mind that what you do or sell cannot be directly compared with any competitor, price will not be an issue. Jewels are not bartered for bricks.

The closer your business matches your competitors the more crucial your Service becomes.

Managing the seemingly insignificant

It is the little things, the seemingly insignificant, that have the greatest impact. That extra bit of clean sand around the base. A 'please' and a 'thankyou' in the right place. That is what separates one brick from another. After all, aren't the bricks really the same?

Peak performance in Service?

Last year I was working at a conference in Adelaide. My schedule was such that I had already worked the day of my flight and when I arrived at my hotel after nearly six hours travelling (including taxi rides) I was feeling pretty tired. I knew I was working early the next day and so, feeling and looking very dishevelled, I was ready for bed. A fact that must have been easily transparent to even the most casual observer. I asked for my room at the hotel lobby only to be told that there had been some 'mix-up' and my room was not available. I was ready to be disgruntled.

'Don't worry, Mr Power,' Kylie said (the employee from behind the Service counter), 'I can see you're tired and this is *my* problem and I will sort it out.' Turning quickly on her heel, she disappeared to return only a few minutes later. Handing me my card-key she flashed me a big smile and said, 'When you get to the room I've allocated, I hope you find it to your satisfaction.' I did. To say the room was spacious would be a gross understatement. It was plush, well appointed and huge (my whole family could have had a disco in it – and I have five kids.).

Laying back on the enormous silken covers, I was feeling pretty chuffed. Just then all of the phones rang (there were three). It was Kylie. 'Everything to your satisfaction, Mr Power?'

The way I see it, that hotel employee handled a potentially disgruntled customer, as a peak service performance. Now, I don't know whether it is company policy to automatically give an upgraded, richly appointed room to any dishevelled and disgruntled customer who looks ready to explode. I suspect not. But I do know that the way I was treated reflected favourably upon the entire hotel.

So, what is a peak Service performance?

Peak performances are those times when an employee goes that extra mile *as a matter of choice*. Kylie chose to take ownership of the problem. She *chose* to give me an upgraded room and she *chose* to follow up. I believe Kylie would still have her job at the same salary level had she not done any of these things. Indeed, I have experienced very different receptions at the same hotel chain.

Peak performance, then, is a matter of choice. It is that discretionary behaviour between the minimum accepted and the maximum possible. Employees in the Service industry have enormous scope in the area of discretion. There are plenty of opportunities to go the extra mile. It is this desire to rise above the 'just-enough' behaviour that typifies the peak performer. It is a commitment to their job and to the organisation.

Peak performance, then, is a matter of choice. It is that discretionary behaviour between the minimum accepted and the maximum possible.

The effective manager recognises that while the success of their business is not in the lap of the Gods, it comes close to being in the laps of their employees. Just as we cannot legislate to make people treat each other fairly, neither can we put rules in place to ensure Service Excellence. In the final analysis, the success of any Service organisation relies on the discretionary behaviour of its employees.

The extra mile

Studies have shown that the top two issues affecting customers' decisions to return to an organisation, are personal recognition and Service. This has been clearly demonstrated by many recipients of the Australian Customer Service Awards. One award winner is a hairdressing salon that exhibited excellent Service. Upon arrival the customer is provided with a cup of tea or coffee, made according to preferences recorded on file. They have the customer's favourite magazine laid out in front of their chair, and a money-back guarantee. As an extra touch, they also provide an umbrella on rainy days. One last thing that sets them apart: they do THREE follow-ups to make sure the customer is totally satisfied.

In the final analysis, the success of any Service organisation relies on the discretionary behaviour of its employees.

Action Steps

• Next time you are looking at increasing customer numbers, or doing something that few other business do, try putting time and effort into getting your staff to treat customers for what they are – special, individual people. Make them feel important!

• Creating employee commitment to peak performance does not happen by default. It needs to be fostered, acknowledged and encouraged. There are some things that you can do to begin the process.

Today: actively seek an employee doing the right thing and acknowledge them for it.

This week: listen to an employee's ideas on going the extra mile – and then support them in doing so.

This Month: lead by example. When dealing with your employees, go the extra mile for them.

The platinum rule

Almost everyone has heard of the golden rule. Do unto others as you would have them do unto you. I think it needs revising. The best revision I've heard comes from Cavett Robert, the founder of the National Speakers Association of America. Cavett said, 'Do unto others as they would have done unto them.' Cavett was right. Not everyone wants to be treated the same way. I like beetroot in my salad. My wife, Heather, detests it. If I made a salad unto her as I would have done unto me, she would hate it. I need to find out first what she wants in her salad, if I am to give her what she wants. It is very easy to fall into the trap of thinking that the way you see the world is the way the world is. It isn't. The map is not the territory; it is only your version of the territory. Everyone looks at their map and says this is what I like and this is what I don't. Our job in Service is to the best of our ability to see the map from their perspective – and then deliver Service in that form.

Our job in Service is to the best of our ability to see the map from their perspective – and then deliver Service in that form.

Action Step

• See things through the other person's eyes. Don't give people something just because you like it; give them Service in the way they like it. Always remember everyone is different.

54

CHAPTER FOUR

We Have Contact

Taking the passion out of passionfruit

Passion is important in business. Knowing and understanding your customers' needs should be something every person in business is passionate about. I have always had a passion for making a difference. I just didn't always know it. Now I do. What's more, I know one of the best ways for me to make a difference is by directing my passion toward customers. When I say passion, I don't mean sneaking around in the underwear department. I mean striving to know more about my customer than anyone else does. To know how best to Service their needs. And by filling their needs, to build customer loyalty. What I am talking about here is taking a broader perspective of the person we call our customer or client.

Broadening perspective

I like to know my customer. I like being aware of all the other needs they may have at the time they are doing business with me. I say needs, because needs don't come in the singular. Customers don't have a need, they have bunches of needs. To think that the customer only has one need is very superficial. It's a bit like a psychiatrist

55

looking at a petrified arachnophobia patient whilst saying, 'We'll just get this spider out of your view and your problem will be fixed'. Stupid. Chances are, there'll be spiders somewhere else. (For starters, I have thirty of the suckers keeping me company in my office).

Out of the mouths of babes

The other day my five-year old daughter discovered the ice-cream her grandad had left in the freezer. She immediately insisted on having a chunk of it. No surprises there. What was a surprise, however, was that once she tasted it she didn't like the taste. It was Dark Jamaican Rum flavour. After much moaning, I had an idea.

Needs then, like passionfruit, come in bunches. You just have to look behind the leaves.

'Why don't you cut up some fruit and stick it on top,' I counselled.

From the open fridge door, Stevie-mish (my daughter), yelled back, 'Dad, we've only got a bunch of passions.'

This I had to see. Pulling the fridge door open wider, I could see she was talking about passionfruit.

'Those are passionfruit, honey,' I said, 'and they don't come in bunches, love, grapes do.'

'Dad, Aunty Michele has passionfruit growing in her garden, and they always grow in bunches. You just can't always see them because they are hidden behind the big green leaves.'

I guess she was right. She usually is.

Needs then, like passionfruit, come in bunches. You just have to look behind the leaves.

56

The movie-set customer

If you are really going to look after your customer you'd do well to go beyond what I call 'the movie-set' approach. At face value, those movie-sets look terrific. A closer inspection reveals that the front isn't, of course, the whole thing. They're just propped up 'cardboard' cut outs. All the action is taking place behind the scenes. Many organisations look at their customers in the exact same way. As if they were two-dimensional cut-out figures, with only one need. Organisations that look at their customers in this way are just not getting the whole picture.

People are more complex than that.

You have to go deeper

For every need revealed by a customer, you can bet there are a whole bunch, just like passionfruit, hidden behind the 'leaves'. Customers are people. And all people are well rounded. Not just the ones who frequent King Size Menswear. They all have a range of needs at any given time. It would serve us well to serve them well by looking a little less myopically at customers' needs.

Looking at the whole person

Look at the whole person. I learned this lesson well when I was doing some consultancy work for a community organisation. This particular group worked with young people at risk. Whatever that means, because to my mind all young people are at risk. This particular day, I was sitting in this community organisation's office with the manager and a government official. A bit of a raucous row broke out in the reception area. The manager broke off the conversation to see what was happening. At the front counter, an older youth – maybe in his early twenties – was vociferously angry that the field officer had refused to give him a cheque for some food. To my mind, he did look hungry and in need of some food. After the manager had sufficiently calmed him down, he returned to the office. The official, who was there representing the funding body, sat quietly for a moment. A pregnant pause hung in the air. Then, curtly, he asked the manager why he had refused to hand over the cheque. After all, hadn't that been the reason the agency was funded?

People come to us with a bunch of needs. It is our job to find out what they really are.

The manager's answer should be a lesson to all of us who serve customers. 'If we were to just give him a cheque and send him on his way, we would have only satisfied the perceived need and only part of his problem. People come to us with a bunch of needs. It is our job to find out what they really are. We want to help the whole person.' The community sector taught me a lot about helping the 'whole person'.

Communities, connections and customers

Although the funding dollar is stretched very thinly, and competition for it is fierce, community organisations work as a community. I guess that is why they call them community organisations. They try to use all the connections at their disposal. I found out later that the youth at the front desk ended up getting support from housing, legal, financial planning and drug counselling organisations. Now, I know that your customers are probably not dropouts, social misfits or delinquents. Although they could be. But they are whole people with bunches of needs. Indeed some of these needs are so necessary to your customer that, if you discover them, Service them and make all the connections, you'll have a customer for life.

Action Steps

- Start to look for the associated needs. Stop looking only at the surface wants. Go deeper and become a problem solver.

- Look for creative ways to discover what other needs the customer may have. They won't just tell you. You have to become an investigator and leave no leaf unturned.

Finding creative ways to Service the whole person

When dealing with customers the corporate world is not so different to the community sector. You must, however, ask different questions. A Cameroon Proverb states, *He who asks questions cannot avoid the answers.*

A couple of good ones to start with are, *What other*

needs does my customer have right now? And, *How can I help them fulfil those needs*?

Let's look at a retail example, although the principle works equally well for any organisation. Say you own a bridal shop. It's a fair bet that anyone buying some bridal wear from you is getting married. (Okay, maybe they are a cross-dresser with a fetish for white, but it is unlikely). Asking yourself the above questions, you would see that your customer has many needs right now. Some of these would apply before they have done business with you, and some would apply after. In the bridal example, their needs could be associated with a florist, a photographer, a marriage celebrant, a venue, a caterer, a stationer, a tourist bureau and a limousine company (even a divorce lawyer, but perhaps that's just a little premature – that comes later), to name just a few. With this knowledge you are then in a position to see how you could be of assistance, and make them feel really special and important. Here's an idea that I have seen work.

What other needs does my customer have right now? And how can I help them fulfill those needs?

Firstly, you approach these associated businesses and offer them a mutually beneficial deal. If there is a business that is likely to serve your customer before you do, why not offer them a gift? This would be no ordinary gift, because all parties enjoy the benefits (come to think of it, isn't that the same with all gifts?). As the bridal shop owner you would go to a jeweller and offer them a gift voucher. The voucher would be redeemable at your bridal shop. The jeweller could give this to every customer purchasing an engagement ring. Would the jeweller accept it? Sure, because it adds value and elevates them in the eyes of their customer. Would the customer be happy? You bet. They have just got something for nothing. And everybody loves something for nothing. The really terrific thing about this idea is where the voucher ends up. Back in your shop. With a willing customer holding on to it. You just gained a customer you probably wouldn't have seen otherwise.

It gets better

Continuing with this example, if you now ask yourself, 'Who will benefit from servicing my customer after they leave my shop?' you can build even better customer loyalty. And you can double how special they already feel.

Now you approach the florist, the limousine company or any of the other businesses that would love to Service your customer. Ask them for a voucher redeemable at their business. Will they be happy to give you one? Sure, if you explain that they'll have customers banging on their door.

In effect, you are building a community of non-competing businesses who all assist each other to maximise their growth. Community organisations do this all the time. At the same time

Think about the customer as a person with a bunch of needs, and then seek to fill those needs.

– and this is important – you are providing exceptional Service. You are building a Culture that reveres the customer. You are making them feel important.

61

And better still!

With a little imagination it is feasible for you to give away – in perceived value at least – more monetary worth of gift vouchers than the purchase price of the Service you are offering. Now that is a real win/win result. The point to this community-minded approach is as simple as it is important. Customers have needs, not *a* need.

Think about the customer as a person with a bunch of needs, and then seek to fill those needs.

Perception is malleable

Towards the end of a busy contract, I decided to take some colleagues out for a 'thank-you' lunch. We chose a nice, local restaurant. The restaurant had been recommended by another colleague, who said that the food was delicious, and so I was looking forward to the experience. As it was mid-week we were the only group in the restaurant and so expected, and got, prompt Service. Our waitress was a pleasant young woman, probably still in her teens and quite chatty, which made for a friendly, homely environment. Perhaps too homely. I'll tell you why.

Some homely memories

When I still lived at home with my parents – during my teenage years – I vividly remember quarrelling with my brothers and sisters over who would get to lick the mixing bowl. Amidst all the squabbling, our fingers dipped, stirred and dabbled in many of Mum's cooking bowls. Not the most hygienic situation, I'm sure, but okay amongst siblings. Not so in a restaurant.

Visions of her prodding at the stuffing materialised in my head. Something must have shown on my face, but she obviously misinterpreted it.

Joking with the chatty waitress was fun – until she revealed what might be going on in the kitchens.

'Do you recommend the Tandoori Chicken?' my colleague next to me asked her.

'Oh, I'm not that big on white meat,' she replied. And with a wry smile on her face she added, 'but whilst I'm in the kitchen, I do try to have a little taste of most things.'

Visions of her prodding at the stuffing materialised in my head. Something must have shown on my face, but she obviously misinterpreted it. Leaning closer she whispered, 'Yeah, we try to have a little fun while we're working.'

My imagination, mixed with memories of what friends had told me about their 'kitchen days' was now starting to get the better of me.

Some teenage memories

Well, you know what teenagers are like. One of my friends who worked in a fast food outlet that shall remain nameless told me they used to play football with the frozen chickens just before they…'cooked 'em just the way you like it'. Perhaps that is why they tasted so tender. Another friend told me that they used to stick a foot up the rear end of chickens – one on each foot - and 'roller blade' around the kitchen in them. Skin-less chicken?

Needless to say, for me, the chicken was off.

What your employees say about your organisation affects the way customers think about your organisation.

Now I come to think about it, this could have been a contributing factor in my now avowed vegetarianism. And if this wasn't enough, her finale delivered the final blow. Bending low over the table in a clandestine voice she whispered, 'If you want my opinion...' I didn't. But she gave it anyway. 'I think the Tandoori smells awful.'

I don't go to that restaurant any more. I didn't know it at the time, but I learned a valuable lesson about Service that day. What your employees say about your organisation affects the way customers think about your organisation.

Watch what is said

It is not enough for you to say that you have wonderful Service, or to think you have a wonderful Service, if your customers and employees don't. The real test of your Service is the sum total of their opinion. You set the standard of Service; your customers determine quality, as they perceive it.

I recently saw a humorous illustration, which reminded me of this.

Before a presentation, it is a good idea for me to visit the loos; nipping out in the middle of a salient point for a 'Jimmy Riddle' may just detract from my message. So, there I was at the urinal, when I noticed a sign:

This facility is covered by the (Company name) Hygiene treatment program incorporating the unique (Company Product) sanitiser system to protect you. This program ensures that the highest standard of health and hygiene is maintained for you around the clock.

In permanent ink just below it was hand written, 'So why does it stink so much?'

I hadn't thought about it before. Probably been in too many men's changing rooms. But come to think about it, the place did stink. What's more, I wasn't real sure about the 'facilities' hygiene program either.

The point is this. You may think that you are providing the best

If your customer thinks it stinks…it stinks. And if your staff think it stinks… it really stinks.

Service in the world, but if your customer thinks it stinks…it stinks. And if your staff think it stinks… it really stinks. Remember that the customer's reality about your organisation is *the* reality. Listening to your clients provides a peek into that reality.

If you know what your staff are thinking about you, you'll have a fair idea what your customers are thinking about you.

Action Steps

- Start listening to your own people. Find out what they think of the organisation. Solicit their views.

- Look around for subtle or tell-tale signs that things are not what you would want them to be.

The four second flash

Have you ever stopped to think about how long you give a page of newspaper before you decide you will read anything on that page? Research shows that for the average person it is about four seconds. Most people will scan the headlines, searching for something that interests them. Looking for the WIIFM (What's In It For Me). A few people read everything from cover to cover, but they are in the minority. Even these people priortise their reading. Focusing on the most important headline first. The rest of us judge whether it is worth our time almost solely on the headline.

If you are not doing something to catch your customer's attention immediately, then you've lost them!

Look through the paper and test it yourself. The headlines stop you in your tracks. The headline is critical. Up to 90% of an ad's ability to pull is in the headline. A great ad has many elements but if you don't have a headline, forget it! You've blown your money.

This idea can be extended to many other things. Take books, for instance. I was recently at a presentation where we found out just how much time you probably gave the cover of this book. About 7-10 seconds. And then because you must have been interested (I am assuming this because you ended up purchasing it, stealing it, or at least borrowing it from somewhere) you flipped the book and gave the back cover about another 17 seconds. If I didn't have you then, I didn't have you at all.

Think about the implications for your organisation and its Service delivery. If you are not doing something to catch your customer's attention immediately, then you've lost them!

Action Step

- What does your organisation do in the first four seconds of customer contact? Are you grabbing the customer's attention in a unique and exciting way? Could you do something more?

  Grab your customer's attention quickly, it's the only real chance you've got.

CHAPTER FIVE

The Feeling of Value

I'll make a logical decision – as long as it feels right

Despite what we like to believe, we don't make decisions based on logic. Sure, we back up the buying decision with logic, but first we make the decision from an emotional base. Ever said to yourself, 'I wouldn't go to him, if he were the last provider in town'? Most of us have. Many factors come into play here. How a person treats their people. Something someone told you about the organisation. The owner's abrupt attitude as well as a number of other things. All emotionally based. We like to do business with people we know, we like and we trust.

We like to do business with people we know, we like and we trust.

I recall purchasing some insulation for our home. We got three quotes. The first two quotes were very similar but the third quote was the most expensive. The contractors were quoting for the same amount of insulation in the same areas of the home. So which one did we choose? The last one. Why? Because we liked the way the guy giving the quote politely spoke to us. Was he the best person for the job? As far as I know there is really only one way to put the batts in a roof. Side by side. There is no skill or knowledge needed. Later I recall trying to justify why we had chosen him. We reasoned that because his attitude was positive when speaking to us, he would keep to the time schedule we agreed upon. You can rationalise anything. In reality, any of them could have done that. No, the real reason was that we liked him.

Action Steps

- Look at the reasons your customers do business with you. When talking with customers, focus on the emotional aspects of the sale.

Remember – emotion first, logic second.

Goodwill is like water in a glass

Your Service is only as good as the Service you last provided. Within reason. To a certain extent, people will judge you according to how they were last served. However, there is evidence to suggest that this is not always the case. If it is the first time this particular customer has dealt with you then the Service they received is the Service they expect. If this Service was poor, then that is how they will rank you, and perhaps never return. If, on the other hand, the Service was exceptional, then you will be rated accordingly, and no doubt win their business. The difference comes when you have built a reputation with the customer, then it is not so clear cut. If you continually and consistently offer great Service, the customer will forgive a slip-up and put it down to a one-off. If handled correctly this is a wonderful opportunity to deepen the relationship with that customer.

Every time you interact with a customer, you build small deposits of trust. If nurtured, this relationship can build to such levels that the customer will tolerate even a fairly major 'stuff-up'.

If you don't constantly do something that the customer sees as exceptional value then the level of goodwill drops.

Let me give you an analogy. When the customer firsts meets you he has a reasonably neutral view of your Service – the glass is half full. If the Service you provide just meets expectations, that's fine, the glass stays half full. The customer's view hasn't changed either way. Every time your Service exceeds the customer's level of expectation, some goodwill is added to the glass. Every time your Service fails to meet the customer's expectations then some goodwill is subtracted from the glass.

If a glass of water is left unattended then the water evaporates and the level drops. Similarly, if you don't constantly do something that the customer sees as exceptional value then the level of goodwill drops. So you can see that you can make a withdrawal from the glass as long as you have deposited enough in the first place. One thing to remember, once the glass is empty it is probably too late – you've lost the customer. One other thing. It is possible to provide such exceptional Service that the customer believes they are actually getting a bigger glass. Both you and they will reap the rewards.

Action Steps

- Keep plenty of water in the glass. At the risk of sounding corny; ensure their cup runneth over. Make small and consistent deposits at every opportunity.

First impressions matter most

For a long time, people in Service have known how important first impressions are. They are now even more important. Everything happens so rapidly that even the time it takes to make first impressions is shorter. As a Culture, our attention span is shortening, and there is plenty to reinforce this.

It is now more than ever, critical to make those first precious moments striking and impressive.

Video clips, for instance. If you are old enough to remember the early film clips of your favourite rock star, you will also remember the camera essentially staying on the band for the entire clip. The camera-operator would hold each position for thirty seconds or more. Not any more. Frame changes have progressively sped up. Five years ago the average time spent on each frame was seven seconds. Have you watched a clip lately? Now they have as many as seven changes every second! This conditioning forces people to make snap judgements. Everywhere. The very first words you utter on the phone, the way your people look in the first few glances or even earlier than that – your marketing material – all speak volumes to the potential customer. 'Hello,' says the operator. Impression established. Envelope delivered. Impression established. Door opened. Impression established. Enough said. You get the picture. It is now more than ever, critical to make those first precious moments striking and impressive. This is where you establish your footing. Make a mistake here, and it's all up hill, with little or no grip. But get it right and you've already begun building a relationship.

Get it right – early!

Forgotten souls

Have you ever stopped to think just how much it costs to originally win your customer? The answer is 'plenty'. You probably spent bucket-loads on advertising, locating and soliciting thousands of people only to get a small percentage of them to become your customer. Yet, once we have them, all too often we neglect them. I'm reminded of a story I once heard. This guy dies and is given a chance to decide which he would prefer – going to Hell for eternity or hanging out in Heaven forever. So

Do you know anyone that treats prospects like this? And their customers as well?

that he can make an informed decision, he is given a look at both places. First, he goes to Heaven. It's nice up there, but there isn't much to do. Then he gets a look at Hell. Here he is treated to a wild and fun time, with wine, women and song. He reckons the decision is easy. 'Sorry,' he says to Gabriel, 'I've chosen Hell'.

As soon as he gets down there he is treated horribly.

He's beaten, he is starved and he's worked like a slave in a sweatshop. He turns to the Devil and asks, 'What's going on? When I first came here, I was treated like I was special.'

'Ah,' replies the devil 'But you were a prospect then.'

Do you know anyone that treats prospects like this? And their customers as well? We should be treating our customers like gold, because that is what customers are – gold.

How can we do that?

Your database is invaluable. Once you have a customer and you have captured their details on your database, you have your most willing and best source of business. If your customer is happy with your Service once, chances are real good that they would want more. If not the same Service, they may want a Service that complements it. People like to be informed and educated, not sold. By contacting your list regularly and giving them information of value, you build a huge level of trust. This is true of your current and your past customers.

Harness the unlimited amount of information available and provide it for your customer.

Harness the unlimited amount of information available and provide it for your customer. The danger is thinking that just because it is common knowledge to you, they know it as well. This is the curse of assumption. What do you know that your customers would value? If you sell tyres, what about, 'Five ways you could increase the life of your tyre', or if you are a dentist, what about, 'Three things you should avoid eating, like mouldy bread, Brussel sprouts and children's leftovers'. You get the idea. Truth is, you know a lot more about your business than most people. Share the information. Your generosity will pay you handsomely.

Action Steps

- Keep in contact with your customers/clients regularly, if for no other reason than to ask, 'How are things going?'

- All relationships are built and strengthened over time. Make every effort to nurture that relationship with your client base, by continually offering them value.

Mine your database

People love to get value. Most of the time we give it to them, but then forget to tell them just how much value we have given them. Customers need the reasons why they benefit from our offers. This is an educational process. People like things clearly described – the reasons to buy, how to buy and why to buy now. Think about it. If you can't answer these questions why should your customer?

Customers that have experienced exceptional Service are already predisposed to the benefits you can offer them. They need only to be reminded so that they can benefit again. There are many ways you can do this. One excellent way is to mail to them regular exclusive offers.

Customers that have experienced exceptional Service are already predisposed to the benefits you can offer them.

Now I know that people don't like getting junk mail. I don't myself. However, I do appreciate getting something that will benefit me.

By sending them stuff of value you have a good opportunity of reactivating customers that might have forgotten you exist. If done properly, it makes customers feel special that you have cared enough to take the time and trouble to single them out. Here are some possible offers to stimulate your thinking:

Action Steps

- Offer customers preferential pricing to encourage them to renew their business. Make them aware this is not available to the general public. And then make sure it isn't!

- Give them early notice of sales or specials.

- Give them first preference on offers of exclusivity on limited items or Services.

- Give clear and educational information that assists your customers in understanding the value you are offering them.

- A customer list is a gold field waiting to be mined. It is so much easier to mine in a proven vein than dig wildly anywhere and hope for the best.

Start digging in your database and you will be staggered by the results.

Follow up

After conducting a mail-out, the critical thing to remember is always, always, always follow up with a phone call. Tests have shown that this can increase your conversion rate as much as 300% to 1000%. That's a lot. Make this a genuine call in the interests of providing exceptional Service. This is especially effective if at the time of the call you can add even more value and more Service to the already beneficial offer. In other words, give 'em something for nothing. Most people I know love something for nothing.

When calling people, respect their time. Near the beginning of the conversation say something like, 'Have I caught you at a good time?' If not, ask for a good time to call. Following up shows you care enough to make sure that your customer gets the best available Service. Be genuine, be sincere and have their interests in mind.

Action Steps

- Put systems in place to ensure that you follow up all contacts and that each follow-up adds value in some way. Always have a reason to follow up.

- When following up, respect people's time. Ask permission to continue the call, and then make it worth their while to give you that permission.

Reverse and reveal the risk

Ask yourself this question: If someone came into your organisation and received poor Service that clearly did not live up to their expectations, would you do something to make it right? Say 'Yes'. If you are in business for the long run, and you put any value at all in your Service, then the answer is always yes. The point is this: Why not let the customer know that up front?

Whenever anyone enters into a transaction, one party feels like they are taking most, if not all, the risk. From the customer's viewpoint, they usually think it's them.

Whenever anyone enters into a transaction, one party feels like they are taking most, if not all, the risk. From the customer's viewpoint, they usually think it's them. Of course, this isn't really the case, because if they are not happy, it will probably be you that carries the financial loss.

So why not take this fear away from them? Tell them openly and up front that you will happily refund their money, replace the item or whatever it takes to ensure they get not just satisfaction but exceptional Service. Make it easy for them to decide to do business with you.

Another way to eliminate the customer's risk is to offer a free trial period. If you work in the area of big-ticket items, you could offer to do a little bit of the project for free. Or if you really want to impress the customer, offer a double-your-money-back guarantee. This has a lot of power.

Sure, you will get some people who exploit your goodwill. But they are the same people that gave you a hard time anyway. They are a drop in the ocean compared to the goodwill you generate through your exceptional Service.

Action Step

- Make it easy for your customer to do business with you. Boldly state that you'll take all the risks. Explicitly mark out what your guarantee means.

CHAPTER SIX

Faster, Higher, Stronger

Stay centred to the inner compass

Some lessons in life leave a marked impression. This lesson was destined to be one of them. It was a beautiful sunny day. The wash of azure blue sky was textured with an aimlessly drifting cloud or two and a smattering of little white, circling dots. I recognised the dots as the small aircraft that buzzed around the aerodrome. Little did I know that I would soon be falling from the sky in one of those little white dots. I was nineteen at the time and excited about the prospect of becoming a pilot – something I

> *Little did I know that I would soon be falling from the sky in one of those little white dots.*

had dreamt of for a long time. I'd saved hard the money I earned labouring.

Finally my day had come. Today was my final, practical examination. If I passed this I would be let loose to buzz freely around those summery skies. From the direction of the hangar, I could see the examiner approaching. All he needed was the music from Top Gun and I would have sworn it was Tom Cruise swaggering towards me. With the music *Highway to the Danger Zone* playing in my head, I boarded the little two-seater Piper. After the preliminary checks, I gunned the throttle and the engine roared into life. I suppose in terms of the Top Gun aircraft I would have had about equivalent power to their starter motors. Still, it felt good to me. We rolled out onto the runway and again I opened the throttle but this time I let the brakes off and the plane lurched forward. As the plane lifted smoothly (well as smoothly as a winged eggbeater masquerading as an aircraft can), I felt in control. Following the directions of 'Mr Cruise', I put the little plane through its paces. That was pretty easy. Until, that is, I was to tackle the 'hood' test.

The fearful hood test

The hood test is an ingenious device, designed to completely put the fear of the Gods into you. At some 4,500 feet and flying at a speed of about 120 knots the examiner (bless his cotton socks) effectively takes away your external vision. And that is the best thing that happens to you that day. The examiner flicks down a black hood over your eyes. Immediately, your other senses get a wake up call. All aircraft to my knowledge are equipped with a number of auditory as well as visual warnings. In the plane I was flying in – no, falling in – the

So, what do you do when you are in a total spin and nothing seems to be going according to a normal plan?

beeping sound ringing in my ears signified that my plane was now experiencing the aerodynamic thrust of an egg. Couple that with the uneasy feeling in my stomach (which was trying to eject my lunch) and you have the feeling of total and utter disorientation. A bit like returning from the buck's night of an alcoholic. Who owns a brewery. Okay, so now my head is spinning, my stomach is churning and my other internal organs are playing musical bobs. I know I have to get myself out of this. 'Recover,' says Mr C somewhere from the haze, as he casually flicks up the hood. Now I am really disorientated.

So, what do you do when you are in a total spin and nothing seems to be going according to a normal plan? Aren't you in the same situation when a customer comes in ranting and demanding, 'Something better be *done* right now, or somebody's going to be!' Well that somebody was me, right now. Let me tell you, eggs drop at

Eggs drop at around 500 feet a minute. A plane with the aerodynamics of an egg drops at about… the same speed.

around 500 feet a minute. A plane with the aerodynamics of an egg drops at about… the same speed. Either way, the results are the same.

When things like this happen, you don't pull out the policy manual. That won't save you. You have to rely on something else. Praying is an option, but in this situation, it too gives unreliable results. The only way to survive is with an inner knowing of the right thing to do. Where does this inner knowing come from? Drill, practice and controlled exposure. This is that stuff that builds Culture in an organisation.

My overriding motivation at that moment was to get the plane flying straight and level so that we could all come out of the dive feeling like we had conquered it. And alive. At these moments, guidance won't come from your instructor. It must come from your gut (or something else might). You want your staff doing the same thing. I spent many hours practicing for that moment and it paid off. You can get the same results with your staff.

Look to the internal compass

The point is to have an internal compass conditioned from drill and practice and from living the idea in your visualisations. A compass that will centre you. It could save your life. How does this relate to Service? It does so because Service Culture has to be a part of you. It mightn't save your life, but it could save your livelihood!

Action Steps

- Live and breathe the kind of Service you want your people to live. Make the Culture one where Service Excellence is 'the way we do business around here'.

- When under pressure, we are most likely to revert to an inner knowing. You want your inner knowing to be one of total Service to the customer. A knowing that the customer wants, more than anything, to feel important.

- Through training, practice, drill and prepare for challenging situations.

Raising the bar

In my house, Saturday is Little Athletics day. That's the day when a lot of little kids run around knocking things over, throw around various shaped objects and grunt a lot. Same as the rest of the week really. Only semi-formalised. At the same time a bunch of parents hang around pretending they know what they are doing, and grunting a lot. Also the same as the rest of the week. If you can stand back from it,

> *Service is often a lot of people scrambling about, looking busy, but not really knowing what they are doing.*

it's really a funny sight. A lot of people scrambling about, looking busy, but not really knowing what they are doing. Come to think of it, that is like many of the organisations I see too.

Who monitors What?

At Little Athletics the parents set up and monitor to ensure things go according to plan. A bit like management in most organisations, really. This is a good thing, because left to their own devices, kids will do the darnedest things. Javelins make great spears. But what really interested me were those kids clustered around the high jump. In the grand scheme of things, they were pretty orderly. A couple of kids scramble around each pole, pushing up the fitting that held the end of the bar. They were trying to achieve a reasonable setting of the high jump bar. All the while, some kids would stand back hollering advice on its height.

As I watched the kids doing this, I couldn't help thinking of parallels to many of the organisations I had worked with. The kids setting up the bar were the management. So, where do you reckon they set the bar? Yeah, so high that few, if any, of the kids trying to jump it could succeed. Instead of jumping the bar, most kids did one of two things. Some didn't put any effort into it (demonstrated by the way they ran at the bar). In effect, they just fooled around. Others just plain gave up (and went back to tossing the javelin at their little sisters). Sometimes a tussle would take place and the ones doing the actual running and jumping (the workers) would get a crack at it. It was now their turn to set the bar. Where did they set the bar? Yep, so low that it took only a little jump to clear.

Little Athletes in the work force

How does this mirror organisations? Think about the Service in most organisations for a minute. If the managers give their directives on the standards and they don't consult with the staff, they'll set them too high. If, on the other hand, there is no commitment or ownership on the part of the workers, the workers themselves set them too low.

Unsatisfactory results

Either way is unsatisfactory. If the children had to set the bar up themselves, chances are they would like to set it where it best meets their needs without regard to any other criteria. I watched small children do this. At the beginning of the day, before the games begin, the children place the bar at a height they know they can easily clear. This is all well and good, but it doesn't stretch them. They really don't know just how good they could be and, most importantly, they don't how they stack up when it comes to the competition. This can happen in organisations too.

> *They really don't know just how good they could be and, most importantly, they don't know how they stack up when it comes to the competition.*

How should it work then? Seek commitment on where to set the bar. Everyone needs ownership. People want to feel good about their successes, but they need to know what constitutes a success for that to happen.

So too, it is with Service

In Service, we often do the same thing. We raise the standard just enough for us to comfortably clear it. We deliver the parcel on time. Not ahead of time. We return the call when we have to. Not as a follow up courtesy. Customers pick up their goods. We don't take it to their car.

We place the Service bar just high enough to get by. At the end of the day, we are not challenged and the customer is not delighted. And the Culture of the organisation has suffered.

Customers may not tell you outright where they want that bar, but chances are they want it higher than it's set.

Who is deciding where to place your bar – you, your employees or your customers?

Action Steps

- Actively involve all of your people in setting the bar. Openly discuss where it is set now and how you can push it higher.

- Always remember the bar can get higher. Communicate this idea to your people at every opportunity. The height of the bar is a direct reflection of the Culture of the organisation.

The high bar just got higher

The year was 1968 and as the world watched, Dick Fosbury changed forever the way athletes executed the high jump. After Fosbury won the 1968 Olympic gold medal in the high jump, the U. S. coach, Payton Jordan, commented, 'Kids imitate champions. If they try to imitate Fosbury, he'll wipe out an entire generation of high jumpers because they all will have broken necks.'

Another expert got it wrong. Generations that followed Fosbury didn't break their necks, but the bar had been set at a new record.

Fosbury went over the bar head first and backwards. He took a chance and he changed the way people think. Forever. Nowadays, no high jumper worth his salt would even dream of jumping the bar using the old scissor leg method. The public expect athletes to continually go higher, faster, further.

Athletes in Service

A similar thing has happened in the world of Service. Not so long ago it would be okay to wait fourteen days for delivery of your goods. It would have been acceptable to be told to take a seat and wait for your turn. These days we want it now, or better yet, yesterday. We live in a world where communication zips around the world in nano-seconds; beamed into our homes through televisions and radios as it happens. Such a world does not tolerate delays. Domino's pizzas promises us 'in thirty minutes or its free', Blockbuster video guarantee if they don't have your choice of new release video now, its free.

We live in a world where communication zips around the world in nano-seconds...Such a world does not tolerate delays.

Successful Service means taking your business to new levels. Customers' expectations are higher. Ignore those expectations at your own peril.

Forget the scissor kick action and instead be prepared to leap higher.

Action Steps

- Recognise that we are in a changing world and that we must embraces those changes. To achieve this we need to adopt the Olympiads motto: Fortius, Altius, Citius – Faster, Higher, Stronger.

CHAPTER SEVEN

Make a Difference

Butterflies and battering-rams

It amazes me that even the smallest things can have the most profound impact. I once worked with a community organisation that found volunteer work for people interested in doing something

> *It amazes me that even the smallest things can have the most profound impact.*

for their community. I recall one man who later had a profound effect on giving purpose to my work. I remember him well. He was an unassuming man, in his mid-fifties and not at all articulate. In fact, he had a terrible stutter. He came by the organisation hoping that he might be of some use to somebody, anybody. We had no trouble placing him, with or without his stutter. There are always community groups crying out for help. The most sought after criteria are; someone that breathes, and someone with a positive attitude. This particular individual had at least one of the necessary criteria. Let's call him Nick.

Customer driven community group

The focus of the organisation was customer driven in that we wanted to meet his needs. Right now, that didn't seem too difficult. All he wanted was something to do. Nick was looked after with due respect and sent off to the awaiting community group. Some time passed and we heard no more from him. Why would we? He was just another customer who we had helped in the course of our normal work. About a year later, Nick came back to my office asking specifically for me. Nick came in and I recognised him instantly, but somehow this time he was different. This time he carried himself with more pride, there was a spring in his step. Confident and self-assured he held out his hand. I shook his firm grip and asked him to take a seat. Nick looked at me intently before speaking. I felt that there was something important he wanted to say. There was.

'Mr P-Power,' he said.

'Terry,' I interjected, noticing that his stutter wasn't quite as bad as I remembered it to be.

His face beamed again. 'Terry, I want to thank y-you.'

'For what?'

'For saving m-m-my life.' He now had my full attention.

'What do you mean?'

'L-let me explain.'

The tale unfolds

I settled back in my chair to listen while Nick told me his story. It was a sad story. He had no family, no friends and nowhere he really called home. He was a loner. He told me how he'd grown up in a series of 'one-horse' country towns. Always treated differently from other folk. Sometimes loathed, sometimes tolerated, but always different. Nick was on a disability pension with no meaningful work to speak of. Drifting from town to town he finally found his way to the city.

The slogan promised a station with 'no more ridicule, no more hurt and no more put downs'. In his heart, he yearned for such a place.

Ironically, here he felt he'd never been more alone. So alone in fact, he began to question whether he might not go to a better place. He had listened to the slogan of Sonshine FM, a Christian radio station. The slogan promised a station with 'no more ridicule, no more hurt and no more put downs'. In his heart, he yearned for such a place. He was ready to take his own 'useless' life. Somewhere deep inside though, he saw volunteering as a last ditch attempt to see some light. He had persevered through the phone-call, he had endured the humiliation and he had come forward.

Holding back the emotion that welled up inside of me I asked, 'And now?'

'N-now,' he said, 'now I have a n-new family.'

And he had. The community organisation he was now with held him in high regard. For he was a dedicated worker, committed to helping others. Nick could empathise with the lonely and the sick, he had been there himself. He knew what it was like to hurt, and now he knew what it was like to feel good. He knew what he preferred.

I'll never forget the words he uttered before turning and leaving my office. He said to me, 'Terry, p-p-pain is invisible, b-but it is very real.'

Action Steps

- Never underestimate the impact you have on others. That call you are taking could be having a huge effect on the person on the other end of the line. What may seem little to you may well change another person's world.

- Always remember that small things can have a ripple effect. Like a pebble cast into the millpond, the ripples made from small acts of kindness radiate outwards, ultimately touching many lives.

Even the smallest thing can have tremendous impact on the viability of the entire operation.

Science supports the effects of little things

A friend of mine spends a lot of time thinking about butterflies. No, he is not a bug-watcher. Actually, he is a consultant who draws heavily on Chaos theory. Chaos theorists believe that even the smallest action can have ramifications of enormous magnitude. Much of their work is based on the discovery of meteorologist Edward

Lorenz. Studying global weather patterns, Lorenz concluded that tiny effects on one part of our planet can and often do affect the other side of the globe.

He entertained the idea that even the gentle beat of a butterfly's wings in Brazil could cause a hurricane in Indonesia. This became known as the butterfly effect.

Similarly, the butterfly effect can work in any organisation. Even the smallest thing can have tremendous impact on the viability of the entire operation.

Too many people look for reasons why things won't work. They are so busy finding reasons why they can't do it that they get stuck.

McDonalds, for instance, uses the idea of up-selling or bump-selling, which now contributes millions of dollars annually to their profits. They didn't invent the idea but they have certainly capitalised on it. Have you ever been in a McDonalds and not been asked, 'Would you like fries with that?'

I doubt it, unless the staff member was just about to get the sack. McDonalds found that when asked that question, four out of every ten people say yes. In real terms, this represents millions of extra bags of fries sold. They recognised that people have more than one need.

Some organisations don't even give it a chance. 'Well that wouldn't work for us because…,' they say. And then proceed to give you a litany of reasons why it wouldn't work.

Too many people look for reasons why things won't work. They are so busy finding reasons why they can't do it that they get stuck. They then try to batter their way through. After a while, using your head as a battering ram becomes tedious.

Stop bashing your head against the wall and fly anyway. Every small beat of your wings makes a difference.

Opportunity hides behind mistakes

Had I chosen to say nothing and pretend that it didn't happen, I would have won the battle. But at what cost?

Every mistake is an opportunity in disguise. People will forgive you for making a mistake; they are less likely to forgive if you don't admit it.

By admitting your mistake, not only will they forgive you; often you will earn their respect. I recall one time when I was sitting on a board of directors when one of the other directors put a motion to the floor and I corrected her on a technical issue.

'You can't put a motion right now,' I said.

I could tell she was unsure that I was correct, but she withdrew her motion anyway.

Her obvious doubt got me thinking. After the meeting, I looked up the constitution only to find she had been right all along. Now I was in a position of choice. I could either forget the whole thing or I could do something to correct my mistake. At the next meeting I publicly made known my error and asked if her motion could be re-instated. Following the meeting she pulled me to one side and said, 'Thank you. I hold you in very high esteem for what you just did. '

Had I chosen to say nothing and pretend that it didn't happen, I would have won the battle. But at what cost?

Studies have shown that up to 94% of customers will come back if you effectively correct an error.

When you make a mistake do you try to gloss over it, or do you see it as an opportunity to win the customer over?

Action Steps

- View every mistake as an opportunity. An opportunity to build credibility and trust with your disgruntled customer. They will not only thank you for it; they will also tell others.

- Go through your records and see what mistakes you have made. And then seek to put them right. And put them right, whatever the personal or organisational cost. It will pay dividends in the long run.

The Kokoda experience

I once walked the Kokoda Trail. One of the most gruelling walks I ever ventured out on. The distance is deceptive. It is approximately 93 kilometres from start to finish. Ordinarily, I could cover such a distance in a couple of days relatively easily. However, over that distance

At the time, I wanted nothing more badly than one of those cavernous valleys to open up and swallow me.

the walker ascends and descends some 18,000 feet. That's a lot of stairs to climb – especially when there aren't any. To put things in perspective, at one point in the trail you can stand in one village and look across the valley to the next. The trip by helicopter takes only 90 seconds. On foot, it is a six-hour, incredibly gruelling hike. The jungle is dense, the insects intense and the climate oppressive.

Looking back it was a barrel of fun. At the time, I wanted nothing more badly than one of those cavernous valleys to open up and swallow me. Instead, the only things that nearly did were the damn insects. Not to labour the point, but there's one thing you need to understand about trudging through New Guinea jungle: it is hard work! In some places, we needed machetes to cut through the thick undergrowth and in others tweezers to remove the leeches. And that was the best part.

The climb upwards

From the top, the view is breathtaking. From the top, I knew every step was worth the effort.

I was reasonably fit, and yet every muscle in my body ached. Climbing the steep muddy inclines, I hoped against hope, as I looked skyward, that a break in the jungle canopy would miraculously appear. Anything to signify that we had finally reached the peak. It is amazing how a glimpse of a crest could rejuvenate me. With renewed effort I would climb to that peak only to find… that it was a false crest. Once over the crest, my only reward was to see yet another incline – densely covered in jungle – rising skyward under a canopy of thick trees. But ah! The pain, the anguish, all quickly forgotten once I reached the crest. From the top, the view is breathtaking. From the top, I knew every step was worth the effort.

That lesson has stayed with me, and I have applied it to many areas of my life. Not the least of which is my absolute Service mentality. Now when I am trying to solve a problem for someone, I persevere until I achieve the desired outcome. Along the way I often reach false crests – I think the solution has been found – only to find another incline over the ridge. But, when I finally deliver the Service I set out to deliver, I feel triumphant, like the time I stood triumphantly upon the crest of the Stanley Ranges of New Guinea. I quickly forget the effort and bask in the reward of a job well done.

Action Steps

- Be aware of false crests, and know that with perseverance you will eventually reach the summit.

- Keep the bigger goal front-of-mind at all times. Focus on the final outcome – a satisfied customer.

Going the extra mile

On yet another travelling adventure, I found myself again in new territory. This time in the heart of the New Guinea Highlands. A fascinating place. While there

I recall being hopelessly lost. An easy thing to do where there are no street signs, or for that matter no streets.

I discovered that parts of this region were only explored as recently as the middle of the Twentieth Century. Once you travel to this region, you understand why. It is a most inhospitable environment and is extremely difficult to navigate. Yet this gives rise to an interesting paradox. For while the terrain is among the most challenging I have seen, the people are 'easy'. People go out of their way to make it as pleasant as possible.

Often what we do for the customer costs us little, but can have a dramatic effect for them.

I recall being hopelessly lost. An easy thing to do where there are no street signs, or for that matter no streets. Aimlessly walking along I saw a New Guinean walking some distance away, and in the opposite direction. He obviously noticed me, because he came across to talk. Many people in New Guinea speak a hybrid language called Pigeon English. Probably a good name because it is as if the people there peck around trying to find a word that has any semblance of being understood. Fortunately for Westerners, they manage. I struggled to tell him where I was heading. As I looked at him, I finally saw some lights going on. He pecked around a bit, but I understood that he knew where I wanted to go. At that moment he turned around and motioned for me to follow him. He was going to take me there himself. Now that is literally going the extra mile. For him it didn't seem like such a big deal. For me it was everything.

People do go the extra mile

Doesn't a similar thing happen when a customer wants something from us? If we put things in perspective, often what we do for the customer costs us little, but can have a dramatic effect for them. Sometimes we need to remember this. Sure, not every customer is going to be exceedingly grateful. That doesn't mean you cannot enjoy the journey yourself. Often it just requires us to take the first step. There is no way of knowing just how great the rewards are going to be.

Action Steps

- Think of ways you can go the extra mile. Talk about these ideas in staff meetings and post successful stories up for people to see.

- Place a 'Win' board where customers and staff can see the milestones achieved by your organisation. This helps keep your people motivated in going the extra mile.

CHAPTER EIGHT

Do The Right Thing

Integrity in Service

Integrity is a key element in peak performance. In the corporate world, integrity in customer service really counts.

When I was a boy, I used to love spending time with my Dad. It didn't matter where it was. Even being at work with him was fine. I especially liked going on private jobs with him. My Dad was a plumber. Not the most glamorous of jobs, but certainly vital. He used to work in and around all sorts of interesting and wonderful places (which I will leave to your imagination). Not sure I'd find them so wonderful any more. Some things just lose their intrigue. Some things stay with you forever. Dad's lesson on integrity was one that stayed.

On some jobs, we'd climb into attics and under floorboards to fit or fix pipes and other plumbing fixtures. It was always fun. The more I went along with him, the more responsibility he would give me. I remember being really excited when he let me loose with the oxyacetylene. I learned that just because you can't be seen, doesn't mean you can't do plenty of damage. I don't know why he got so mad. His hair grew back.

In fact, I learned many lessons crawling around those dark cellars and creepy attics. My Dad, you see, took pride in what he did. Back then, I had never read about customer Service (at least not with a capital 'S'). But if Service means integrity to work, integrity to your customer and integrity to yourself, then I'd sure seen it.

My Dad taught me more about integrity than any textbook. Although he never spoke about integrity, he sure had it. Once, we were working in a dark cellar deep within the bowels (sorry, couldn't resist) of an old but 'well-to-do' house. I asked my Dad a question that seemed innocent enough at the time. The years of time have not eroded the power of his answer. I asked, 'Dad, why are you always so concerned about getting the joins so neat and the pipes so perfectly vertical or horizontal?'

What do you do behind closed doors? Do you ask the question am I doing this right or am I doing the right thing?

Putting the flame to one side, he stopped what he was doing and turned to look quizzically at me.

'Well,' I continued, 'no one is ever going to see it. Nobody is ever going to crawl under here and take a look. No one would ever know if it were done messily or done right.' He looked deep into my naive eyes and said, 'Son…I'd know.' Then he looked away and picked up the spirit level. That's integrity.

What do you do behind closed doors? Do you ask the question am I doing this right or am I doing the right thing?

If the company is clear, everyone is clear

The reverse is also true. If a company espouses a view that states, 'We care about our customers', then they'd better start caring about their employees first. Incongruent messages beget incongruent messages. Few things

Few things infuriate people more than double standards.

infuriate people more than double standards. It is an exercise in futility to ask employees to treat all customers with the utmost respect, integrity and caring if the company treats it's employees differently. Double standards breed contempt, but worse than that, they breed a cynicism that actively undermines the company. And make no mistake, employees can white-ant even the most robust company. The company must have clearly stated directions in relation to Service and adhere to them themselves – rigorously. The spin-offs of such congruence are many. Given any opportunity – and there are many – your employees will speak positively and encouragingly about how things are done at XYZ company.

Parallel agendas

Almost without exception, organisations run two agendas. Firstly, management and workers say one thing in meetings and AGMs. Then there is the hidden agenda. I draw the parallel with something I learned at university. When I was studying for my Post-graduate Education Diploma, the lecturer spoke about something he called the 'hidden curriculum'. The hidden curriculum covered all those unsaid things that go on in schools, the unwritten rules that guide the ethos of the school, which all the students know and follow. Even when they are never written down. The teachers and administration staff follow them too. What am I referring to? Let me give you some examples that I discovered during my short foray into teaching.

The hidden curriculum covered all those unsaid things.

Written rule: This school offers an exciting extra-curricula activity program. Parallel hidden rule: the school shall be cleared of all staff and students at 3.05PM. Written rule: All our students are to be nurtured and treated with respect at all times. Parallel hidden rule: Morning tea breaks are a time for discussing poor behaviour of students and parents in a derogatory and uncomplimentary way.

Written in invisible ink

Are these 'hidden curriculum' rules written down? Of course not. These rules are not politically correct, complimentary or positive. They are, however, very real. More real, in fact, than the school quadrangle. Kids know these rules. Teachers know these rules. Admin know these rules. They contravene everything the education system stands for, but they permeate every classroom, every corridor and lurk behind every corner.

Expose these rules to the light of day. Scrutinise and recognise them for what they are: Demoralising, harmful and counter-productive. Who needs to do this? Everyone. Who needs to make the new written rules? Everyone.

106

Parallel agendas in parallel sectors

I see the same thing every day. In workshops around the country, I hear of the same double standards. They exist in corporations, community groups and the government sector. And they really get up people's noses. All this talk about *the customer is always right.* Hogwash! *Staff are respected and treated fairly and with dignity.* Hogwash!

Steve Simpson, an expert on customer service, calls these 'unwritten ground rules', or UGRs. The UGRs are *the way we do business around here,* and if they are not aligned with the message going out to the customers, you have a recipe for trouble. Employees treat customers the way the company wants the customers to be treated, provided that the employees are treated the way they want to be treated.

Action Steps

- Work hard to expose the 'hidden curriculum' in your organisation. Enlist everyone in this worthwhile goal.

- Ask yourself: 'Is this rule about doing things right? Or is it the right thing to do?' These are very different questions.

- What behaviour are you modelling to your employees? Are you working on the business or just working to show busy-ness?

107

- Act with integrity. Align the things you are doing with your beliefs and inner self. People can easily tell when you are congruent and sincere, and are more likely to reciprocate in kind. Centre yourself in your own competence, and be true to yourself.

- Be prepared to follow through what feels right for you. Trust your personal confidence. Trust that what you have done is good enough, and don't buy into perfectionism. Trust in your team, and in the job you have delegated to them. And then, when you catch them doing something right, praise them.

- Put your mistakes on the table and by doing so turn them into an opportunity.

Feelings, not logic drive the mind

One of the essential ingredients in any Service relationship is just that – the relationship. Companies that work with people (which means all of them) are in the relationship business. People first make decisions about you based on how they feel. If you or anyone you know has ever uttered the words, 'It just didn't feel right', then you know what I am talking about. People do want a quality product, but before they even get close to that, at some subconscious level they first check in with their feelings.

As human beings, we like to believe we are rational animals. Yet, I know I have avoided a shop because I didn't like the manager. He may well have the best price and the best expertise, but to buy from him just wouldn't feel right, so I go elsewhere. Illogical, but reality. There is an electronics retail shop near my home, but I never shop there. As many as three years ago, I went in to this particular shop to buy a good quality Walkman. The shop assistant offered me good Service. I thought she had clearly understood what I required. I paid my money and walked out a happy customer. Only for a short while.

He may well have the best price and the best expertise, but to buy from him just wouldn't feel right, so I go elsewhere. Illogical, but reality.

When I got home I unwrapped the walkman and plugged in the headset. The sound was clearly not stereo. I fiddled with a few knobs. Listened again. Nothing changed. Thinking I might be doing something wrong, I decided to go back to the shop and check it out. The assistant had gone to lunch so I spoke directly with the manager.

'Not a problem,' he said, 'You just need this little adaptor for the headphones.'

'Great. Thanks,' I said, getting ready to walk out of the shop.

'That'll be one dollar ninety five cents,' he said.

'Sorry?' I questioned.

'That'll be one dollar ninety five cents,' he repeated. I was incredulous. I had just spent hundreds of dollars believing that the purchased item would do the job I asked for. Which it didn't. Now the manager wouldn't even make it right by giving me the one dollar ninety five adaptor. I paid the one dollar ninety five. He lost thousands in revenue. I have since spent a lot of money on communication technology and software. None of it from him. When I left his shop, I didn't feel good.

Interestingly, until recently I would still go to his shop. Not to buy, just for advice. He does know his stuff. I won't buy from him, because his attitude stinks. If he had taken the time and effort to build a relationship with me – that would have started with a one dollar ninety five cent give-away - he would have had a lot of my money. Not to mention all the people I tell about his business. Oh, by the way, I don't go to him for advice any more. The shop is closed.

Action Steps

- Feelings are the foundation for a good relationship, and a good relationship is the foundation for good business.

- Look for small investments to make the customer feel good. A give-away earpiece is a good start.

Making the work easy

'It was a good job the banana wasn't loaded,' my wife joked, when I finally got to speak with her. No, I wasn't going around the do-dally-twist – as my Mum used to say – but I could have been if I wasn't using a banana. You see, only moments before the 'banana incident' I had just listened to one of my staff take a particularly challenging call. One of those special customers, you understand. As soon as I had walked into her office, I could practically taste the tension. I wanted to defuse it quickly. As I was on my way to the staff room at the time, a banana was the only thing I had handy. Instinctively, I crouched down, reached for the banana and yelled, 'Anyone moves and the crazy one gets it.'

My staff member – now looking down the pointy end of a Colt 45 banana – did the only thing possible. She burst out laughing. Mission accomplished. I knew all those years of training would pay off one day. After she stopped laughing I sat down with her and talked the

> *Instinctively, I crouched down, reached for the banana and yelled, 'Anyone moves and the crazy one gets it.'*

incident through (the angry customer, not the banana thing). What could have easily been a very difficult situation was defused with humour. Humour ranks as one of the greatest Service tools known to humankind. Humour can soften an unhappy staff member, and, if done well, a customer too. Humour makes people feel good, it creates a bridge between otherwise quarrelling people. And besides all this, it makes work easier as well as fun.

What is a Culture without humour?

A colleague and a great friend of mine, Steve Wells, has a wonderful philosophy in business and life. He says that *if it seems too hard then you are doing it wrong*. Ironically, I had lived this philosophy in my previous businesses and organisations, but had failed to apply it to my training/consulting business. When I took that advice on board, everything fell into place. Once I stopped thinking about how right or how wrong I was, and began focusing on making it fun, it became easy and effective. While running Service workshops I was so focused on content and processes that I forgot to make it fun. The results I got were fine, but I knew I could get better. Besides, it was such hard work.

In a sense, it is hard to define fun. Everyone's idea of fun is different. This much I do know. When I loosened up, lightened up and let go, the workshops were a hoot.

In a sense, it is hard to define fun. Everyone's idea of fun is different. This much I do know. When I loosened up, lightened up and let go, the workshops were a hoot. Now everyone enjoys themselves, takes something useful away with them and comes back for more. I reckon that is a real win/win.

The fun factor

My feeling of having fun while I Serve is transferred to the people I work with. I experience the same thing every time I receive extraordinary Service. There is no doubt about it. People giving good Service enjoy themselves. Sure, it manifests itself in many ways, but I reckon you can sum it up as fun. I have said it before but it is worth repeating. Good Service is a transfer of feeling. If you are having fun it shows, and chances are your customers will loosen up too.

Don't make it hard on yourself, have a little fun.

Actions Steps

- Look for ways to encourage fun in your workplace. Build into the Culture an attitude that makes it all right to have a laugh and a joke.

- Reward humour that is tasteful and inoffensive as long as it is not counter-productive. Good humour rarely is.

CHAPTER NINE

Learning From The Future

Probable, possible and preferred futures.

Futurists cast their gaze forwards with a multitude of options. Apply the same idea to your Service. This means that you can see the future of your organisation in many ways. Let's look at these options one at a time. The first is *the probable future model*.

Probable future

Applying this kind of forecasting to the way you provide Service gives us some interesting insights. Cast your eye forward along a continuum, with the future as simply a continuation of the past. A linear projection. If you keep doing business the way you have always done it then you can expect more of the same. While this will not provide you

This is the poorest approach. There are too many factors for the future to be an extension of the past.

with a very accurate prediction – because of the changing nature of Service and the world in general – it will provide a general picture of where you are heading. Down the tube.

In my opinion, this is the poorest approach. There are too many factors for the future to be an extension of the past. Who could have foreseen how computers affect our daily lives? Just the other day a carpenter friend of mine told me that, 'Without computers, I just could not do my job.'

This model has served us well in the past. It will serve us no longer.

With this in mind lets look at another option - *the possible futures model.*

Possible future

This forward thinking requires a broader perspective. Takes into account the changes you see around you and incorporates them into your vision. You know that customers are no longer satisfied in the way they once were. So look at ways to ensure you meet their changing needs. You will probably not only survive, but also prosper. Those that fail to recognise this will, probably, no longer be in business. This type of thinking gave us 'the decade of the customer' in the nineties.

It began to dawn on people that today's customer is more demanding, more informed and less tolerant than ever before.

It began to dawn on people that today's customer is more demanding, more informed and less tolerant than ever before. The emphasis shifted away from mass production to customised needs.

This is a fair approach, but in my opinion, the third option is better; that is *the preferred future model.*

Preferred future

In taking the preferred future approach create the vision exactly how you would wish it to be. If you would like a twelve-hour turn-around visualise how that could happen. If you would like every Service provider to be friendly, courteous, informed and always willing to go the extra mile, envisage that now. If you desire every customer's expectations to always be exceeded and for every customer to be left in awe at the level of your Service... create it now. You may not obtain this lofty ideal, but by envisaging it now, you could get close. Building a vision, if done well, creates a

One thing is for sure; you will miss one hundred percent of the chances you don't take.

positive, constructive tension between now and the future. A powerful vision has pulling power, like a giant magnet. It gives you something to continually strive for. Again, in the words of a great friend of mine, Steve Wells, 'Paint the picture exactly as you would like it.' His advice is always good.

One thing is for sure; you will miss one hundred percent of the chances you don't take. To create a Culture that other organisations envy, you must start now.

Action Steps

- Set up a planning day. Bring together all your key people and discuss the preferred future. Visualise it in specific, meaningful and exciting terms.

- Time line when you want to achieve these things. Put up a visual representation of the goal. Make it compelling and discuss it often.

- Have a vision of magnitude. Make it a BHAG (a Big Hairy Audacious Goal). The original goal of IBM was, 'World peace through world trade'. That's pretty hairy.

The possibility approach to planning

The challenge with any kind of planning is to break free of the mind-set that reflects our current status. When I talk about future visioning, people often get stuck. They are immovable because they are trapped into their current level of thinking. To move beyond that we have to stretch our possibility thinking, without losing track of our current situation. It is important to know your current status. I understand that. It is also important not to be so bogged down in reality that it stops you looking beyond. In planning, if you stay with the present, your thoughts and ideas are hamstrung. Focus only on the

To move beyond that we have to stretch our possibility thinking, without losing track of our current situation.

future and you risk your thoughts and ideas becoming unruly animals impossible to tether. Those that live *only* for tomorrow are dreamers who live in a fictitious world that is never going to materialise. What personal development expert, Denis Waitley, calls, 'Someday isle'.

A better way

The art is to shuttle back and forth between these two points. As you traverse this territory you will begin to see the gaps to take you to a new level. By doing this, you construct a creative tension between where you are and where you want to be. Contrary to popular belief, tension is good for you. If it is a healthy tension. A tension with enough energy to get you motivated. Enough tension to get you up early and keep you up late. A burning desire to achieve your dreams. This tension creates the pulling power necessary to draw you towards a preferable future. A future where the Culture of your organisation is exactly what you want it to be.

As you traverse this territory you will begin to see the gaps to take you to a new level.

Create creative tension.

Action Steps

- Cultivate your ability to shuttle back and forward by using your greatest power. Your imagination. Einstein, no less, said, 'Imagination is more important than knowledge'. Make sure you give yours a regular workout every day.

- Depending on the size of your staff, either get all the key players together, or gather a representative group and begin to brainstorm your ideal preferred future.

- Solicit ideas from your customers, vendors, directors, managers, contractors, and all other staff (including mailroom staff and cleaning staff). Consider all ideas seriously.

- Change any linear thinking in your organising to possibility thinking. Challenge the mentality of, 'That's the way we have always done it', with new ideas.

The silly question

'Always the beautiful answer who asks a more beautiful question.'
– e. e. cummings

I have heard some damn silly questions. Many of them from customers – 'So, does the red one over there come in...red?'

I have often heard it said that the only silly question is the one that goes unasked. I disagree. I don't know about you, but I have heard some damn silly questions. Many of them from customers – 'So, does the red one over there come in...red?' I think we all have a tendency to ask silly questions, at times. Cases in point are the questions we ask when seeking feedback.

120

Chances are you will get what you ask for. The mind is a very complex thing. Yet, it does have some aspects that are predictable. For instance, the mind will seek what you ask of it. There is a familiar exercise that many speakers use to illustrate this.

Try this exercise yourself. Firstly, look around the room where you are reading this book. I want you to notice everything you see that is blue, everything you see that is red and everything you see that is green. Now close your eyes. Remembering hard now, I want you to recall everything you see that is... grey! How did you go? If you are like most people in my seminars, you will have difficulty remembering the grey objects (except, to my chagrin, my grey hair – I hate that!). The reason is clear. We see more easily that which our mind focuses upon. I have seen this lived out many times. One of my most memorable impressions was the time one of my nephews was learning to ride a bike.

The fatal ride

He was about five or six at the time. Marc (my nephew) was starting to get the hang of riding. My brother had done the bit where you run alongside them holding on. Marc was now getting to the stage where he could go it alone. The next step was out to the footpath. Picture this. My sister-in-law, my girlfriend and I all standing by the brick letter box waiting for the moment when Marc would ride solo. Further up the path we could see Marc just being released from the safety of

We see more easily that which our mind focuses upon.

my brother's grip. He had done it. He was now on his own. One thing you need to know: this was a particularly wide path with absolutely no objects to hit. Except one. The brick letter box. What we did next practically ensured that Marc's safety would be doomed. As Marc wobbled uncertainly down the path we began shouting in a steadily increasing crescendo, 'Don't hit the letterbox,' and, 'Watch out for the brick (very solid, very hard) letterbox.' Almost

Almost immediately like a homing missile on command, Marc veered toward the letterbox. Crack! Fortunately, the letterbox was repairable.

immediately like a homing missile on command, Marc veered toward the letterbox. Crack! Fortunately, the letterbox was repairable. I am not sure about Marc's bike or his ego. A more appropriate thing for us to be shouting would be, 'Stay closer to the grass,' or, 'Aim for me.' At least then the letterbox would still be all right. The fact is we move toward that which we focus on. We find that which we seek. And our brain finds the answer to the questions we ask of it.

The upshot of all of this is that if you ask a question like 'What do you dislike about our Service?', watch out for the answer, because you have effectively asked their brain to start searching its database for anything it did not like. That can be very dangerous, and detrimental to why you asked in the first place. I found this out in my own training business.

Action Steps

- Always focus on the outcome you do want. Not the outcome you don't want. This simple shift in focus can have a dramatic effect on results achieved.

- Similarly, ask questions that keep customers thinking about the things they like. You will still get the other stuff, but it won't be their major focus.

A lesson learned

As a builder of Service Cultures, feedback is just as important to me as it is to anyone else. It is how I receive that feedback that makes the difference. When I first began exploring the idea of shifting organisational Culture, I gave out feedback sheets. My logic was simple. That is what other consultants did. I quickly realised that this was not the best approach. I was seeking concrete, constructive criticism. What I got was a load of warm 'fuzzys'. People only told me what they thought I wanted to hear.

My logic was simple. That is what other consultants did.

I wanted stuff I could use to improve my Service, so I began asking the question, 'What didn't you like about my consulting?' Whoa! Was that the wrong question to ask? This achieved a focus on the negative, and if you look hard enough for something, you will find it. Yes, even in my course people found something to whine about; 'The breaks were too long',

123

'There was too much food', 'The handsomeness of the presenter distracted me from the excellent information.' Okay, I wrote that one. You get the idea.

I changed my approach. Now I ask, 'What can I do to serve you better?' This focuses attention on what I did well and what they would like more of. In doing this, the negative takes care of itself, without being the focus of attention.

Action Steps

- Question the questions you ask. Start looking at what and how you ask your customers if they are getting what they want.

- Remember to also ask the right questions within the organisation. Get in the habit of always framing questions and statements in the positive. Instead of, 'Don't forget to ask for the (you fill in the blank)', say instead, 'Remember to ask for the (blank) '.

- Remember that asking, 'What didn't you like?' *is* a silly question.

Fluidity is better than solidity

I have treasured watching my five children grow. They are fascinating to watch. Their ability to persist in the face of adversity is truly amazing. As proud as I am of my children, I know that this ability is not unique. At least not in children. All babies love learning and love the challenge. They get up from their first feeble attempts at walking. And fall right back down again. They get up. They fall down. Until eventually, they stay up. They don't stop to analyse the process. They just do what needs to be done.

As we get older, most of us lose this resilience. Instead, we analyse each setback, call it failure, then give up. The danger is that we then fail to move at all. We get stuck in 'paralysis by analysis'.

Better to have a clear picture of where you want to go and then take a step towards it. Any step is better than no step at all. Children know this. We should learn from them. The worst that can happen is that you go the wrong way, or fall down, and if you do, make a correction and continue on. In taking that step, you're better equipped for the next. Moving toward a Culture of excellent Service must be a conscious and decisive decision.

The prime mover effect

I like to think of a Service Culture as a juggernaut of potential like a hugely powerful prime mover. If there is no change to improve things, this prime mover will just tick-over. It will just sit there and idle, until eventually, it runs out of fuel. Sure, the prime mover is working but the results are less than satisfactory. However, once you get that machine moving, once you get past the inertia, a Culture of Service can take your company places that you only dreamed of. But first you must get the wheels rolling. It begins with a single turn.

Action Steps

- Take the first step. Then keep moving. It need only start with one small thing. Any one thing suggested in this book would be a good starting point. The idea is to get some motion happening.

- Encourage positive steps in everyone. Keep directing people along the right path.

- Provide constant feedback. Let people know they are on the right track.

- Reward generously along the way. People need positive rewards like a fish needs water. Without it, they suffocate.

- Books and industry journals are a great source for discovering Service trends. Listening to tapes in your car is another way to maximise the effectiveness of your time. For the most part, commuting is down-time. The tape player offers a virtual university of know-how and learning. Again, I know this is not new. Yet, surprisingly, few people maximise the potential of their mobile university. Put a tape or CD in your car and play it, its that easy!

- Public and industry specific seminars are often a great investment even if you take away only one or two practical and immediately useable ideas. The Internet, too, if used wisely, is a great tool. For some free articles to get you started check out: www.execedge.com.au

- Seek new knowledge at every opportunity.

  Always keep learning.

CHAPTER TEN

The Wisdom of Customers

Don't assume they'll tell you

Dealing with the public can be hazardous. There is a risk that customers won't necessarily tell you what they want. Assuming that they will is very dangerous. I did some work in an organisation that illustrates the psychology behind this.

Practically the entire office floor talked about one man as the proverbial pain in the rear-end. Yet, by all accounts, he flitted around oblivious to the fact. He simply acted as if he was 'Mr Popularity'. As a consultant to this organisation it didn't take me long to work out exactly who this person was. Why didn't he know?

Because no one told him. Would his behaviour change? Without any feedback, it's unlikely. I finally spoke with this guy. He was totally unaware that some of his behaviour was getting up people's noses. His comment was, 'Why didn't someone tell me?' Fact is, most people won't tell you what they don't like about you. At least not to your face. The same is true of your organisation.

There is a risk that customers won't necessarily tell you what they want. Assuming that they will is very dangerous.

Ever been in a restaurant where the food tasted pretty ordinary, and the Service wasn't much better? Sadly, it's a pretty common occurrence, but an understandable one.

'Why didn't you complain?' I asked. 'He wasn't really asking,' she said, 'he was just doing his job.'

Not so long ago my wife and I went out for a celebratory dinner. One glance at the menu and I had a feeling the experience wasn't going to be that wonderful. We had chosen a restaurant that we'd heard was pretty good, but because we are vegetarians, I had called ahead to ensure they could cater for us. They assured us that it would be no problem. However, when we looked at the menu it was clear that there was nothing vegetarian at all. I called the waiter only to be told, 'Not a problem, the chef will rustle up something creative for you'. It was creative all right. He had pushed the meat off a plate of meat and boiled vegies. I was just about to say to my wife that we ought to complain when the waiter returned with our drinks.

'Everything to your satisfaction?' he chimed.

My wife said 'Fine thank you.'

'Why didn't you complain?' I asked.

'He wasn't really asking,' she said, 'he was just doing his job.'

Encoded responses

Isn't that the perception we often get? It is as if we have these conditioned responses that are genetically encoded at birth. The person serving you says, 'Everything fine?'

You say, 'Yes thank you.'

End of discussion. You know they are not really asking and they know you are not really answering. And that is where the customer feedback ends. As a society, we are just not very good at giving people honest feedback. Too many of us have learned from bitter experience that when we complain we find that 70% of the people don't care and the other 30% are glad. But revenge is sweet. Because while we are not good at telling the people who may be able to do anything about it, we sure are good at telling anyone else prepared to listen.

No sooner do we step one foot out of the restaurant than we turn to our partner and say, 'Won't go there again, food was lousy.' I know, because we did.

It doesn't stop there either. We'll make a point of telling a bunch of other people as well.

You know what the really crazy thing is? Research shows we will keep on telling other people for up to twenty-one years. Imagine that,

When we complain we find that 70% of the people don't care and the other 30% are glad.

someone griping about your organisation endlessly. For more than two decades! Ridiculous. By the way, if you are interested in the name of that restaurant just drop me a line. I'll be glad to share it.

Turn 'em around through questions

The good news is you can turn this around if you are willing to make the effort. It begins by asking the right questions. But we need to find more creative ways of asking those feedback-type questions. Questions asked in retail outlets are a classic example of the benign interactions carried out every day of the week. If you were a fly on the wall at almost any shop this side of the black stump (in some shops you'd be fighting for your place), and watched the interactions, you would see the same scenario played out ad-nauseam. A customer walks into the shop with an assistant hot on her trail.

'Can I help you?' the assistant parrots.

And the answer? Yes, you already knew it…

'Just looking, thanks.'

One non-existent relationship. Customers will give this stock standard reply even when they are not 'just looking'. Fact is, it's a silly question. I read about one organisation that experimented with changing the questions they asked. Nothing else, just the questions. The result was an incredible upswing in sales. Instead of asking, 'Can I help you?' when a customer walked in their shop, they were trained to ask, 'Hi, have you been in here before?' Without thinking, some customers answered, 'Just looking, thanks.' Then they realised that it was a real question. A real question requiring a real response. In effect, this enabled the shop assistant to open the conversation and the relationship.

Find creative, innovative and new ways to find out the customers true feelings

If customers said, 'No', the assistant could then say, 'Welcome, let me show you some of the things we have on offer.' If they said, 'Yes', the question became, 'Great to have you in the shop again, what brings you back this time?' Then the customer can answer… 'Just looking, thanks.'

Find creative, innovative and new ways to find out the customers true feelings.

Action Steps

- Not all questions are good questions. Test and measure which questions give the best results. Test and measure which questions make customers feel the most important.

- Create a Culture that encourages experimentation with questions. Remember to put an element of fun into the questions.

Gossip is good for business

Talking about you behind your back is gossip. Gossip is the worst kind of disease. Sadly, it's rampant in many organisations. No matter how many organisations I work with, I am still amazed by the proliferation of gossip. Walk through practically any organisation in corporate Australia and you will find people in little clandestine cliques surreptitiously gossiping about a raft of issues. The boss's scented letters from the mailroom, the performance of the mailroom, the people in the mailroom. In fact, almost anything you can imagine. Listen closely and you will hear these same people saying, 'The thing I hate about him is the way he talks about you behind your back.' Crazy.

However, like any negative in life, with a little imagination, it can be put to good use. Even glue that won't stick can be put to good use. Just ask the people at 3M. You know, they are the folks that gave us those little sticky notes.

If people are 'gossiping' about you – and believe me, they are – then it makes sense to capture what they are saying. Don't assume that everything they say is without value. In these hidden corridors people talk about stuff that has a direct bearing on organisational processes and Service. I've said it before, but it warrants repeating. People won't tell you, but they will tell others. Especially if the questions are framed in the right way. The right way is to put processes in place that make it easy to tell others. I know it's a dream come true for some people, but pay someone to listen in on their conversations. That's what we consultants do. Someone from outside is more objective in their listening. This will give invaluable insights into what customers – both internal and external – are saying. With a few simple questions, an outsider could find out more about your Service in a few hours than you could in months.

I know it's a dream come true for some people, but pay someone to listen in on their conversations.

Action Steps

- Become more aware of what people are saying, and more aware of how this could impact your organisation's performance.

- Find an objective ear. Seek someone with a proven track record for sniffing out the gossip and turning it into an action plan. If you're stuck give me a call.

Being listened to is better than being heard

Once they have told you, act! In listening to people as a consultant I am amazed how often I hear the comment, 'Nothing will come from this'. Sometimes people are telling everyone that breathes about poor Service. Secretly they are hoping something will change. Rate-payers do it about their local government, staff do it about their management and customers do it about Service. Seems everyone is complaining to someone. Except the people that can make a difference. Complaints are out there. Real and apparent to everyone – except the organisation. Like a bore at a party – everyone knows he's

Every complaint is a golden opportunity to keep that person talking. Our aim should not be to shut them up.

a bore except him. Every complaint is a golden opportunity to keep that person talking. Our aim should not be to shut them up. It should be to get them talking. Don't just hear them. Truly listen. Show you are listening by acting on their suggestions. I know that not all their suggestions will be smart. But unless we actively listen, we just won't know. Chances are, if they are miffed, others are too.

Listen and then act!

Action Steps

• Advice is useless unless acted on. This applies to

feedback. If feedback is worth taking, it is worth acting on – as soon as possible. Put into practice the suggestions and win advocates. Have them talking for you, not against you.

- Surprise those people that said, 'Nothing will come of this', first with your actions and secondly with a thankyou note. Or perhaps even a small gift. After all, they have just guided you to the next level.

Your people are your greatest asset

B-Digital is a highly successful company operating in Perth, Western Australia. They sell mobile phones. In a period of only 18 months, this organisation grew from a staff of eight to over three hundred. A phenomenal growth. To the customer a mobile phone is a mobile phone is a mobile phone. So why the remarkable success? Put simply, their people.

Steve Mitchinson, the company's Customer-Service manager (at the time of writing he had been promoted to Customer Relationships Manager, and had been awarded the Call Centre Manager of the year) takes a pro-active approach to customer care, which is even reflected in his job title – B-pro-active manager. He recognises the value of looking after his staff so they in turn will look after the customer. Examples of his initiatives to keep staff motivated include: contracting masseurs to give massages to his staff while they are at work, buying pizza en masse, and bringing hot-dog vendors right into the office to celebrate the fourth of July (even though this is an *American* holiday). He also offers all his people nationally recognised training and qualifications at his expense.

Shifting the focus

Focus as much on your own people as you do on your customers. If you want your staff to provide exceptional Service – and you do or you would not have read this far – then you have to understand the prime motivator for all human behaviour. It is encapsulated in the acronym – WIIFM – What's In It For Me. This is not a new idea. We have known for a long time that people are motivated by What's In It For Me. This is not some sad indictment of the human race. It is just a reality. A built-in survival mechanism. People are always asking themselves that question at a subconscious level. If the answer is 'Nothing,' then why should they do it? The answer is, they won't. They may pretend to provide Service, they may appear to be caring, but ultimately they have another agenda. The key is to find that.

What's In It For Me. This is not some sad indictment of the human race. It is just a reality.

Positive effects

It's amazing what a positive effect little things have on people. A colleague said that he regularly took his staff out to the Pizza Hut. The cost to the organisation was next to nothing. Especially when compared with the impact on morale and productivity. Your people's morale is in direct relation to how important you make them feel. High morale is vital to maximise the performance of your people. It affects every facet of their performance. Without it, the feeling of success will always elude your team no matter how high their salaries. High morale is the cornerstone of any successful organisation. One of the best ways to create it is to lead by example.

If you want to enhance people's contribution to work, play to their motivation.

I have done a considerable amount of work in the community sector. During this time, I worked with many volunteers. Without exception, they had some motive for doing what they did. This is not to detract from the good work they were doing. Far from it. Rather, it says that if you want to enhance people's contribution to work, play to their motivation. It is exactly the same with paid staff. People have to be shown how they will benefit if they are to buy into a Service Culture.

Action Steps

- Find out what motivates your people. And give it to them. Remember that all people want to feel important. The way to find out what is important to them is to tune into their WIIFM.

- As Steve Mitchinson says, 'Reward and recognise all staff at every opportunity.'

- **Honesty:** Always promote honesty by leading by example. If you say you are going to do something, then do it. This is not only good modelling, it is good time management practice. Ultimately you will only commit to those things that you have time for. Make your word your bond.

- **Response-ability:** That is, the ability to respond, ably, in any situation. Promoting responsibility for your own actions sends a clear message to others that they too should hold themselves accountable for the job they do. By taking responsibility, people are less likely to blame the system, the organisation or the technology. Instead, they will look for solutions.

- **Risk:** Take risks and be prepared to accept the consequences. Create a willingness to go with the unknown. Allow creativity to flow through and around you. Reward risk-taking as a part of growth. Be prepared to step into the unknown with your people – you never know what you might find.

- **Listen:** Listen, not only to others, but also to your higher self and your purpose. Listening to your inner self will build trust with your intuition. Value yourself for who you are and what you are right now. Encourage others to do so also. Don't seek the approval of others; seek the approval of yourself. Then, and only then, will your motivation become intrinsic.

- **Self-Honouring:** Respect everything you do. Reward yourself for tasks well done, irrespective of the significance of the task. Don't wait until the job is completed; honour and reward yourself every step of the way.

- **Creativity:** Look for and find unique and interesting ways to reward yourself and your staff.

- High morale and self-esteem are contagious. In the final analysis, honesty begets honesty, respect begets respect and trust begets trust. The best managers don't just manage – they lead. And this makes people feel important.

CHAPTER ELEVEN

Hidden Strengths

Seeing with new eyes

New employees are often terrific at making mistakes. I love that. They make errors because they are not locked into a narrow perspective of 'that's the way we've always done things'. They have no history. They notice things so obvious that you want to slap yourself in the face. (Okay, sometimes they make such bad mistakes you want to slap *them* in the face.) If you can get past the urge to give them a clip around the ear every time they ask one of those silly questions – as we said before some questions are just plain silly – and listen to why they are asking the question, you could learn something. I know I did.

> *They notice things so obvious that you want to slap yourself in the face.*

I once managed an expanding organisation that had a steady inflow of entry-level employees. This can be a double-edged sword. One side of the blade delivers a blow to operational smoothness. It takes time to train someone and energy inducting them into your workplace. The other side of the sword, however, is an asset in helping to cut through new ways of doing things. The fact is, new employees see things through new eyes. They are looking at the same things but they see them with a breath of fresh air.

A child's view of the world

I liken this to how children see the world. One of the great joys of having children is the rediscovery of things you had begun to take for granted (like sleep). Hardly ever does a day go by without at least one of my children shouting for me to come and look at something. And insisting that I come no matter what I may be doing. I could be up on the roof taking the air conditioning covers off – it happened to me only last week. Children create a sense of urgency. After clambering down from the roof, I am coaxed to my knees.

One of the great joys of having children is the rediscovery of things you had begun to take for granted (like sleep).

'Look Dad, this spider's got tiny yellow spots all over its back.'

After I get rid of the urge to throttle my son, I view the spider with a new sense of admiration. Only moments before, had I seen the same spider in the duct I would probably have squashed it. I think some managers tend to have the same approach to their new employees.

The new employee's view

'Who is this cockroach coming in here saying 'take a look at this?' Ever known anyone with this attitude? If we choose to step on these 'cockroaches', we have just done ourselves a huge disservice. These people often bring insights overlooked by people with many years more experience. Why? They are not trapped in set ways of thinking. The challenge for many organisations is that they are so caught up in the way they do business they don't stop to look at other ways of doing things. I always made it my business to spend time asking these people how we could improve our Service and was rewarded for my efforts by many simple, innovative ideas.

A simple idea

An example springs to mind. I once had a new staff member who noticed that returning faxes was a nuisance because of the way they operate. Faxes work with the print face down, where you cannot see the number you are dialling. She

The challenge for many organisations is that they are so caught up in the way they do business they don't stop to look at other ways of doing things.

reasoned that if this was a little irritating to her then maybe it was for our clients. She suggested we have our fax number printed on the back of forms that were to be faxed to us. This simple idea made it just that little bit easier for our customers. As a result of this initiative our response rate to faxes increased measurably. Although she could not physically see the frustration experienced by our customers, she had seen it in her mind's eye.

A cost saving idea

There is another reason for listening to your people at the coalface of your organisation. They are not blind to the obvious. Familiarity breeds contempt; the unfamiliar

143

breeds awareness. I remember reading about a case in point. In many of the great Japanese car factories, the philosophy is to listen intently to suggestions from those on the shop floor. One day a worker was walking around the plant on his maintenance routine, when he was struck with an obvious question. 'Why are the lights on in this factory?' Ordinarily, that would have been a stupid question – how else could the workers on the production line be expected to see? His question, however, was anything but silly. There were no production workers, only robots.

Ordinarily, that would have been a stupid question.

He took his question to the management who listened and then did something even more important. They acted on his observation. That section of the factory now runs in low-level subdued light, only lit up for maintenance purposes. The company saves tens of thousands of dollars on utility bills every year. Such action breeds a Culture where workers and their ideas, are valued.

An idea ignored

The reverse of this strategy reveals the stupidity of not listening to people who actually do the job. I was doing some consulting in an organisation that administered concessions on certain kinds of vehicles. For the customer to claim such a concession they had to assert that the vehicle would not be used on government roads. A fair enough thing. No real problem there. The problem arises when management are not flexible enough to listen to the workers...

144

One workshop participant told me that he had – because of policy – been doing some really trivial, time-wasting work. A submission had come in requesting concession on the basis that the vehicle would not be used on the road. This man had to write to the person making the request, explaining he could not get a concession until he could prove he would not use the vehicle on the road. The vehicle was a 187 tonne excavator! In the same week, he had to write to another customer who asked for a concession for a drilling rig. Policy demanded he send a letter explaining that only drilling activities enjoyed this type of concession, and could the customer therefore state the intended purpose of the equipment. In my experience, not many drilling rigs are used for chauffeuring brides around.

The problem arises when management are not flexible enough to listen to the workers.

Take another look through the eyes of novices and your workers on the shop floor, and then listen and act.

Action Steps

- Pull out all your policies and get them viewed by novices. Let them ask lots of questions and if you don't have good answers for the policy, throw it out.

- Welcome new people into your organisation and

show them that it is a Culture that encourages suggestions. Look at all suggestions with an open mind.

The front line knows best

Ignoring suggestions from front line staff is tantamount to sticking your head in the sand. I once saw a cartoon that best illustrated this. The scene is a medieval battlefield, and the captain is pushing away a soldier with a sub-machine gun, saying, 'I haven't got time for new inventions, I've got a war to fight.' The person doing the business every day is often likely to have ideas about doing it better.

It is at the front line where managers learn too, just being involved in the daily operations of the business.

Many of the staff couldn't even tell you what the CEO looked like, let alone having talked to him.

Bob Ansett, who virtually personified Service, recognised the value of this. Ansett had all of his executives spend one day per month working at the front counter, just so they could keep their finger on the pulse of the organisation.

In the book, The One Minute Manager, Ken Blanchard emphasised the need for managers to be seen by all staff. He advocated what he called 'walk about management'. The Chief Executive Officer literally walks around the organisation asking people how things are going. The CEO shows no bias toward higher-ranking staff or areas of preference.

I was reminded how important this is when I was

146

doing some consulting in an organisation recently. Many of the staff couldn't even tell you what the CEO looked like, let alone had talked to him. And those that did know him said he ignored them in favour of other sections that he favoured. This caused enormous friction between the sections. This could so easily have been avoided, had he taken the 'walk about management' approach.

When a customer is speaking with you, right at that moment, you are the company.

Listening to staff and encouraging them to put forward their ideas is quite simply good management practice.

What ideas do your staff have that could make you money, save you resources or create efficiencies?

Ask your staff what improvements they can make – and then support them in their efforts.

The face of the company

It happened in the bank, but it could have happened anywhere. I had been waiting in the queue for about six or so minutes and was now getting close to the front. At first, I could only hear bits of the conversation. Soon I would be able to hear it all. 'What do you mean I'll have to go to the other desk? I have been waiting in this line for an eternity.'

The teller responded quietly and politely. But it wasn't good enough. The customer was now at explosion point. 'You give me the #!%&'s! **First** you send me a letter telling me I had to come in, **then** you make me queue forever and after all that **you** have the bloody gall to tell

147

me I'm in the wrong #%$& line!' Now that bank teller had a choice here. She could have responded by saying, 'Wait a minute pal. I didn't send you the letter, I didn't make you queue up and I didn't make the rules about what I can and can't serve you.' Fortunately, she didn't. She understood a fundamental rule about dealing with customers. That is: When a customer is face to face with you, then you are the organisation. Warts and all.

Rather than seeing this as a personal attack, make it an opportunity to put things right for your company.

The teller responded quietly and politely. But it wasn't good enough. The customer was now at explosion point.

After all, when a customer is speaking with you, right at that moment, you are the company. All the joy or all the angst that customer is currently feeling will be attributed to you. It may be that you have never dealt with this customer before. You may not be aware of the problems or the successes they have experienced with your company.

Right now, in the customer's mind, that doesn't matter. Not one iota. All that matters right now is that they are dealing with you and they want a result. And they want it now. It was unfortunate that I could not hear what the teller was saying. She remained calm and obviously said something that settled the problem very quickly, particularly under the circumstances. I guess she could have whispered to him, 'Shut up or I'm gonna snot you one.' But I don't think so. My guess is she made a decision on the spot to solve his concerns at her counter.

In minutes, the customer's problem was dealt with and he was walking away looking not-too-worse for the experience. Now that was interesting to watch, but it didn't finish there. As the man walked past me I overheard him remark to his wife, 'They're not that bad, you just have to be clear with them.'

Although this may seem irrational, it is the customer's reality. Remember, again, the customer's reality is *the* reality.

I guess she could have whispered to him, 'Shut up or I'm gonna snot you one.' But I don't think so.

Action Steps

- Take responsibility and the customer will respect you for it. Make every employee aware of this, because it is crucial to exceptional Service.

- Make it your goal to ensure all people in your organisation are empowered to make decisions that appease the customer.

- Get every employee to take responsibility for Service.

Beware of the Service expert

The complexity and rapidity of change defies the claim that experts know it all. This is not to say you shouldn't value expertise within your organisation. You should. But be wary of the person who claims to be an expert. The title suggests they have already learned everything they need to know about Service and therefore information transfer can only ever be one way. From them to you. The value is in that person who fosters and reveres curiosity and humility. Claiming expert status is claiming you've already arrived. Look for new and interesting ways to positively surprise your customer.

Action Step

- Don't build a team of experts. Rather, foster expertise.

Sharing your strengths

It is a fact that all people have strengths and weaknesses. People who work in Service roles are no different. If exceptional Service and a Culture of Excellence are your goals, draw out and share those strengths. In a recent workshop, we were discussing how to deal with difficult customers. 'Difficult customers,' laughed Helen 'No problem. Aggressive-types – we give those to Jason; Screamers – we pass over to Dave; and Heavy Breathers – I keep for myself.' Good fun, but not a good strategy. 'That's fine,' I said, 'but what about when Jason and Dave aren't around?' As with most humour, the statement contained an element of truth. Some people are better at dealing with one kind of person and others are better at dealing with different people. The challenge is when you'd prefer a 'heavy breather' and you end up with a 'screamer', you still have to deal with them.

Hidden talents

Amazingly, the knowledge needed to handle most of these problems is easier to get hold of than a heavy breather in an old people's home. They're probably right in your organisation. Look around at your people. Are there a few years experience there? Are there people so good you would personally like to see them experimentally cloned? (and some you'd like just to be experimented on?) So often in organisations I see a wealth of knowledge, experience and skills untapped and left in one person. What happens when this person leaves? A great big hole. Doesn't it make sense, then, to draw out the resource for all to benefit? This is one of the great joys of working with companies.

The challenge is when you'd prefer a 'heavy breather' and you end up with a 'screamer', you still have to deal with them.

Most people are only too happy to share their skills. People generally see sharing knowledge as an acknowledgment of their contribution. As the saying goes, 'emulation is the highest form of flattery'. There is no doubt about it. Some people just handle customers better than others, but if you can get people sharing their ideas, everyone wins – the employee wins, their colleagues win, the company wins and importantly, the customer wins.

It amazes me that some people can work together for years and yet fail to see and use each other's strengths. Yet, given the opportunity in a workshop people are often proud of their abilities and only to willing to give their best and hard-won tips.

Action Steps

- Draw the most out of all your people. Everyone has something of value to offer – even if it's what not to do.

- Have facilitation workshops where the sole purpose is to share knowledge, ideas and skills among your people.

- Give employees opportunities to share ideas.

Experiencing excellent Service

The Chinese have a saying that I am sure many of you would have heard: Tell me, and I will forget; show me and I will remember; involve me and I will understand.

The knowledge needed to handle most of these problems is easier to get hold of than a heavy breather in an old people's home.

A good creed for imbuing a Culture of excellence. People need to experience excellent Service if they are to deliver excellent Service.

A manager in Sydney understands this principle. He said that at practically every staff meeting he would extol the virtues of exceptional Service. This time he decided to do something different. He would involve them. He called a meeting for the usual time. That was where the similarity to his normal meetings ended. When his staff turned up for their meeting, they were ushered to a fleet of waiting limousines. From there, they were taken to a special function room. The tables were heavily and spectacularly draped. There were candelabra in the centre of tables. The room was filled with fresh cut bouquets. At each place setting lay silver cutlery and an embossed place name. On every staff member's table was a gold pen. Engraved on the pen were the words, 'Awesome Service'. And everyone received a personalised, embossed planner. After a sumptuous meal, the manager discussed Awesome Service. Only this time it was different. This time they understood.

On every staff member's table was a gold pen. Engraved on the pen were the words, 'Awesome Service'.

Now this was all pretty extravagant. But did it have an effect? You bet. You may not have the budget or resources to achieve this, but there are many creative ways that you can 'walk' your staff through a process that you want them to embrace.

Action Steps

- Think of some creative way to involve your people to experience what you would like them to deliver.

- Involve your staff at every level, at least in some way. Even at the senior decision making level, consultation and collaboration will smooth the process. People like to feel that they have contributed.

153

CHAPTER TWELVE

A Quality of Mind

Everyone is a person

'Any colour you like. As long as it's black'. Henry Ford didn't make too many blunders in his business career. But if he did, that was certainly one of them. Ford failed to have the foresight of a more discerning public. A reason his beloved 'black, model T' took a dive. Other car manufacturers were not so myopic. However, it is doubtful that even the more progressive among them could have foreseen the relentless march of customer choice. And if one thing distinguishes us from the rest of the animal kingdom –and for some people there isn't much – then it is our ability to choose.

Slugs crawl under wet slimy leaves, because it is a 'sluggy' thing to do. People, on the other hand, crawl under slimy places for the sheer fun of it

Slugs crawl under wet slimy leaves, because it is a 'sluggy' thing to do. Dogs chase their tails because it is a doggy kind of thing to do. People, on the other hand, crawl under slimy places for the sheer fun of it and still others chase themselves around in circles – I am not sure why. But ultimately it is all choice. We need to remember that customers are not slugs or dogs (although you could be forgiven for thinking some of them are!).

155

The main thing is to keep the main thing the main thing

We sometimes lose sight of the fact that those we deal with are people first, and customers second. Customers are not some sub-species of the human form. They eat, breathe, and have demands, likes and dislikes. Just like you and I. And like all people they want to be treated with respect and courtesy. No matter what your business, if you deal with people – and everyone does – then you are in the respect and courtesy business. When people do business with you, they want to know that you are a person too. Choice is no longer an option for people nowadays. It is a given. Everything from cool drink to cars comes in a squillian different flavours, colours and styles. Your point of differentiation is your Service. Countless studies have shown that people do business with people that they know, like and trust.

No matter what your business, if you deal with people – and everyone does – then you are in the respect and courtesy business.

Action Steps

- The first step toward greater Service is courtesy and respect. Exercise it regularly and often.

- Remember that customers are people first and customers second. This is the natural order of things.

- Treat people as people first and as a customer second.

156

Comparing apples with ...tyres?

I was recently in one of those very rare garages where people still actually serve you. The young man pumping the fuel wiped the windows and politely asked if I needed anything else. I told him everything was fine. 'What about the tyres?' he said. I got out and looked at the tyres and sure enough, they looked like they might need a change. It would have been neat if he could have then sold me some. He didn't, but he had alerted me to the fact. The next day I decided to ring around to get a good price. Doesn't everyone? Sure enough I found a reasonably wide price range, and was about ready to settle on a price, but decided to make one more

I was greeted with the usual salutation, but that is where the comparison with any of the other tyre shops ends.

call. The call was to a local company. I expected similar Service. Local it may have been, but it was anything but backwater in its approach to Service. I was greeted with the usual salutation, but that is where the comparison with any of the other tyre shops ends. Instead of just giving me the price, Ryan asked me a series of useful questions. 'Mr Power, so that I can offer you the best tyre for your car, do you mind if I ask you a few questions?' He then went on to ask me what type of car, what do I use it for ; family? Business? What kind of mileage? He then recommended a tyre based on that information. And I have to tell you it wasn't the cheapest. Did I buy it? You bet. I was convinced I wasn't just buying any old tyre; I was buying the tyre for *my* car.

There is competition out in them thar hills!

In business, competition is a very real factor. Having said that, it is worth knowing which area of competition to focus on. Many businesses put too much emphasis on the price and forget those all-important intangibles. Given the chance your customer will ask the price and quickly make a decision based on that alone. Unless you are the cheapest in town, this leaves you in a no-win situation. In order to keep lowering the price you will also have to lower the quality of Service. Once that begins you're on a slippery slope into obscurity. It is better to avoid being compared on price altogether. If your Service delights the customer, in her mind she will no longer be comparing apples with apples. All the rest will be selling her apples. You'll be fulfilling her need for a tyre.

In order to keep lowering the price you will also have to lower the quality of Service. Once that begins you're on a slippery slope into obscurity.

Let your Service raise you above the competition.

Action steps

- Get your people asking questions and moving from order-takers to solution-finders.

- Coach them in the needs of your customer so that they are always striving to fill that need.

Quality assurance has nothing to do with quality

Making sure something is the same every time doesn't necessarily mean that it is quality every time. What those six quality control ticks represent are a company's commitment to procedures. Tom Peters in his book *The Pursuit of Wow!* says it is possible to obtain quality assurance on the making of concrete life jackets. As long as every jacket is within a set tolerance that ensures they all roll off the production line the same, then it can be – theoretically at least – quality assured. The point is stretched a little but it does illustrate the absurdity of only focusing on procedures.

Quality is a perception held in the mind of the customer. Building the perception of quality in the customer's mind has little to do with procedures the customer cannot see. If, on the other hand, the procedures

Quality is a perception held in the mind of the customer.

lead to building this perception, then make this clear to the customer. People love to brag about the effort the provider made. Rolls Royce put sixteen layers of paint on the Silver Shadow. While this makes for a quality product, the most important thing is telling the customer so they can see the quality behind the scenes. After all, you cannot see sixteen layers of paint!

Quality belongs in the customer's mind – keep it there!

Kaizen: constant and never-ending improvement.

Kaizen is a Japanese word for anyone interested in Service to adopt. Loosely translated, Kaizen means *seemingly insignificant, constant and never ending improvement.* Service is after all about the little things. Service is not about revolutionary technological advances; it is not about a new machine that can do things quicker. Service is about people serving people. Sure, technological advances can aid in that process, but ultimately it is how human beings interact with each other that gives a company the Service edge. Little improvements on how we greet customers, how we answer the telephone or show customers to their seat. The good news is that there is always room for improvement. We just need to be open to the idea that there can be improvement.

Service is not about revolutionary technological advances; it is not about a new machine that can do things quicker. Service is about people serving people.

When it comes to human interaction it is a lot easier to get one hundred people making a 1% improvement, than it is to get one person to make a 100% change. A great start would be for everyone in your organisation to find one thing they like about dealing with customers and then share that with every other employee in the company.

It amazes me that so many people want all the change to happen all at once. Mostly, it doesn't work that way. I coach people that if they want to get fit, start with one push-up a day and do that for a fortnight. The common reply is, 'Oh that is too easy.' So you know what they do? Nothing. Those that do the push-up for the full fortnight are then ready to step it up. This is how fitness is built up – in stages. If you want to improve Service, start small, and not with some great scary radical change. Maybe offer a lolly to every child when their parent is talking to you. Not after a sale is made, but before the sale.

Jim Rohn says that when he goes to a restaurant he tips the waiter before the meal starts. That way he is assured of good Service. Give Service first, and your chances of getting Service are hugely increased.

Look for little improvements every day.

A vision to steer by

A company needs direction. People need direction. A direction gives people the drive to do what needs to be done when it needs doing. Without it, people wander about in a daze, wondering what it's all about. (Know anybody like that?) Creating a Culture that exudes customer care doesn't happen by accident. There has to be a vision, which becomes the benchmark for measuring the Culture of the organisation. The vision is an inspirational view of the future. People are not inherently lazy. They just want a reason for doing what they do. Sure, part of the reason is the pay-cheque. But only part.

People are not inherently lazy. They just want a reason for doing what they do.

After working with countless people and asking them what they want from their jobs, it is interesting to note that the pay comes some way down the list. Employees want and need the interaction, the camaraderie and feeling of self-satisfaction that work provides. Employees want to feel that they are part of something bigger than just a job. A vision can provide this feeling.

The vision is the over-arching statement of where the company is heading. The ideal. The utopia of organisations.

Everyone needs to create the vision. A vision without ownership is nothing more than a bunch of meaningless words. Too often, the vision is created from up high with little or no reference or consultation with the employees whom it is supposed to motivate. That just won't work.

For a vision to have any real power involve as many people in the organisation as practical.

The vision is the over-arching statement of where the company is heading. The ideal. The utopia of organisations. This may never be achievable but that's okay. The striving makes it worthwhile. The business guru, Deming, said that, 'No company without a plan for the future will stay in business'. A significant part of that plan needs to focus on Service. Serving the customer is the reason businesses exist. Without customers, there is no business.

Creating the vision, gives the guidance, gets the going happening.

Now you're on a mission

Once you have your vision in place, boldly stated and prominently placed, start your mission to achieve it. The mission sits under the vision. It is still stated in broad

162

brush strokes, but is more focused than the vision. If the vision is what you want to be, then the mission is the vehicle for taking you there. As with the vision, the mission must be all-inclusive to have any real power. Get everyone involved. This takes time but it is a worthwhile investment of time.

Make the mission motivating.

Values underpin it all

It is a pointless exercise creating vision and mission statements without reference to values. Values, whether we realise it or not, are the basis upon which we make all decisions. And like people, organisations have values. The core values of an organisation need to be openly stated. This transparency helps employees and customers alike understand and buy into the philosophy of a company. The values of a company say, 'This is what we stand for'. Values are aligned when a company collectively thinks, says and acts congruently. The heart of the organisation should match the head.

The core values of an organisation need to be openly stated.

An interesting exercise to get people thinking about their values is to hold a mythical dinner party. Imagine you are having a dinner party and you could invite any ten people, living or dead, along. Who would you invite? Once you have your invitation list, ask yourself why you invited these people and what values they embody that appeal to you. This kind of thinking will give you some clues as to your own values.

Now take the values of these people and add any you think are important. Now put them into a hierarchy with the most important at the top. There is no right or wrong priority or list. All values are simply individual choice. Knowing yours and other people's values will then help you set the values of the company.

Having set your vision, mission and values, you are now in a position to set some informed goals for the organisation.

Clarity of values is critical.

Action Steps

- Hold a meeting to establish the values of individuals, and by extension the organisation. Begin by writing down everyone's values. Then ask the question "Which of these is most important?" Keep asking the question until you have a clear hierarchy.

- Clearly display the shared values of the company for all to see. Do this in a prominent place.

CHAPTER THIRTEEN

Sending The Right Message

Illogical leaps

Imagine you have just boarded an aircraft and are seated in the chair. You instantly notice that your seat has a wet patch and when you look up you see the source of the leak. A small gash in the cabin lining. Right away, you don't feel real good about this. You call the hostess who moves you to the next available seat across the aisle. From your new position, you can still see the steady drip into your previous seat. Before the aircraft takes off you are given a hot napkin to wipe your face. Only yours is decidedly tepid and looks a little grimy. These two incidents alone would seem insignificant and you sort of brush them off as unfortunate oversights.

You are now becoming less and less tolerant of this airline, and this is when your thoughts take a turn for the worse.

You call the hostess only to find she has already buckled herself in for take-off. You are now becoming less and less tolerant of this airline, and this is when your thoughts take a turn for the worse. I know. Because this is exactly what happened to me. My thoughts started to move along this track: 'I wonder if the hostesses get any training on how to handle this leak if it gets worse. I wonder if it has anything to do with the aircraft's flying capacity. I wonder if their engine maintenance is this

shoddy. In fact, I wonder if the pilot is even qualified.'
Illogical? Maybe. But that is the way the mind works.
Wouldn't you have doubts? As it turned out the flight
went fine, and I have since looked into their safety track record and it is surprisingly good. But I won't fly with them again.

Forget to say thank you and you are totally ignorant. Fail to offer someone a seat and you are incompetent.

The same thing can happen in your organisation. Forget to say thank you and you are totally ignorant. Fail to offer someone a seat and you are incompetent. One act is linked to the other, not through reason but through emotion. If you think that what you are doing can be misconstrued and linked in any way to poor performance, then it probably is.

Action Step

- What little things are you doing that could be improved? Get the little things right. They are the little illogical steps that lead directly to the big stuff.

Points of Difference

Noted marketing expert, Winston Marsh, is fond of saying, 'It is not the best expert (in other words the one who is actually the best at the technical aspects of what they do) but rather the best marketer who will get the most business'. I think he is right. But I would also add...
it is not only the best marketer but also the one who has

the best relationship with their customer who gets *all* the business. The soft skills, as they are sometimes called (ironically, they are really the 'hard skills') are the things that create exceptional Service. They offer your point of differentiation. Marketing will get the people to your door and your expertise will satisfy them once they have decided to do business with you. But the quality of your Service will affect their decision

The soft skills are the things that create exceptional Service.

to do business with you in the first place. And this will keep them coming back. The right Culture is the one that focuses on Service as a key point of differentiation.

Be mindful of where you can create points of difference.

Know their pain

Anthony Robbins, the best selling author of *Unlimited Power* and *Awaken the Giant Within*, teaches us that everyone is motivated by the twin forces of pleasure and pain. People will move away from pain and towards pleasure. The same motivation drives your customers in the pursuit of quality business. If these two forces are pitted against each other it is usually pain that flexes the most muscle. You can do many wonderful things in your business, but if on a number of occasions the customer feels pain, they will walk. Knowing this, we can use it to our advantage. If we anticipate what pain our customers are feeling and then work to alleviate that, we will woo customers our way. This is effective positioning. And positioning should be part of the Culture.

167

Doggy doos and does it well

I mentioned before that my son, Cameron, was asked to create a low-overhead micro business and decided to sell pet bricks. I asked him why anyone would want to buy them. 'That's easy, Dad,' he replied, 'I know how much you hate cleaning up our dog's 'doo', and I bet everyone else does too. I'll just tell people that with this pet you'll never have to clean up mess again.' He sold out on the first day. I understand that there was an element of humour involved in these purchases. However, he did clearly position his product with something many people could identify with. Particularly in the area of their pain.

If we anticipate what pain our customers are feeling and then work to alleviate that, we will woo customers our way.

Where are your customers hurting? The time they have to wait? The number of different people they have to deal with, the amount of 'doo' they have to put up with?

The doo I was dealing with

Recently I had to make a call to register some financial software I had just purchased. By the end of the call I was ready to go back to the quill and ledger. The 'doo-meter' was starting to peak. I waited on hold for 23 minutes (I timed it) and when I finally got through I was told I that I had called the wrong department. While on hold I had to put up with their nauseating advertising and false starts.

168

What do I mean by false starts? Have you ever been on hold (is the sky blue?) and listening to that wonderful 'muzak' when a sickly voice comes on to tell you, 'Thank you for holding...' and you quickly jump back to attention. At that moment, you think you are actually going to talk to someone. Then the message continues; '...You are still in the queue'. Aaaaaaah! Makes me want to scream. Okay, so now I am talking to someone and they say, 'Oh, you need to be transferred to what's-his-face'. Three transferrals later and I was getting ready to explode. In exasperation I finally put the phone down. I registered by post.

There has to be a better way. I feel pretty sure that most reasonable people would get similarly miffed by such treatment – including the managers that lead this organisation. I understand that technology is a necessary function of business growth. If done right, though, it need not be a hindrance. It can, in fact be used to alleviate your customer's pain rather than exacerbate it.

By the end of the call I was ready to go back to the quill and ledger. The 'doo-meter' was starting to peak.

Action Steps

- Find out where your customers are hurting. And then take steps to get rid of their pain.

- Find ways to increase the pleasure level. Include as many small things as necessary. Customers will love you for it.

The technological double-take

There is an ironic twist when it comes to technology and Service. While people are becoming increasingly disenchanted with technology on the Service front, there are some people who love it. If you have ever been on hold on a 'customer Service' line where they are saying, 'Press 1 for ...', or, 'Please hold, your call is valuable to us', you are probably one of the masses experiencing pain. On the other hand, technology has the capability to strengthen and create excellent Service. In my line of work I get to stay in a hotel or two, which is not my favourite thing. There are aspects, however, that I do enjoy. It is a nice feeling when you call up room Service and you are greeted by your own name. Many hotels I stay in now do this. How do they do that? Simple. When my call goes through to them, it is also on a screen on their desk, which gives them my details. I see this not as 'Big Brother', but rather as a nice touch. Once upon a time, only hotels had the capability to do this. Now, with 'caller recognition dialling' some innovative companies are doing the same thing.

I see this not as 'Big Brother', but rather as a nice touch.

There is a small pizza shop in Melbourne, Australia that uses this technology to their advantage. When you first order a pizza from them, they take down a few details such as your name and phone number. Alongside this information, they plug in the details of your order. Once they have all this data it is a simple process to get a picture of your preferences. The next time you ring, the computer 'recognises' your number and flashes your details immediately on to the monitor. Can you imagine how important you feel when you dial for a pizza and you are greeted with, 'Good evening Mr Power, would you like your usual, or would you care for something extra today?' This is technological use at its best. Providing pleasure and eliminating pain.

Put technology to use as a Service tool, not a Service hindrance.

Action Steps

- Make technology work for you, instead of you working for it. Contract someone who has expertise in contact management software.

- Install and use any technology that is going to make your customers feel special.

Moments of truth

In his exceptional book, *Moments of Truth*, Jan Carlsson wrote about the importance of every customer contact, no matter how brief. He argued that any brief moment – when a receptionist is asked the time, when a customer is shown through the door, the first words spoken on the telephone – creates a lasting impression of your organisation. At these brief but crucial moments, the customer is positioning your company in a myriad of ways. In ways that sometimes seem illogical. The customer may be thinking, 'Well, if the receptionist can't even give me the correct time how are they supposed to get my order by the due date'. Or, 'They were really courteous when they showed me in, I bet they show that kind of consideration with all my interactions'. Or, 'If that is the way they are going to greet me, they can forget ever doing business with me'. I am not suggesting that people do this at a conscious level. They clearly do not. All of this processing happens at a subconscious level. Haven't you ever walked out of an organisation thinking *I wouldn't want to do business with them.* Your partner asks why, but you just don't know, you can't put your finger on it. However, you do know you are not going to do business with them. This is because somewhere in the dark recesses of

Somewhere in the dark recesses of your brain you have made a connection with something they did. Something that says **warning.**

your brain you have made a connection with something they did. Something that says *warning.* It matters little at what level you processed this doubt. The doubt is there.

On the other side of the coin, this subconscious processing can greatly increase the odds of a positive experience. Carlsson realised this and coined the phrase 'moments of truth'. By embracing the importance of these 'moments', he turned the airline SAS from a multimillion-dollar loss into a thriving company.

Points of contact

The lesson from Carlsson is that every time you have a brief point of contact with a customer it speaks volumes about who you are and what you represent. Each one of these contacts represents a moment of truth – even the aspects not seen with the eye. These moments are critical to your Service Culture. These moments are when you answer the telephone, the first handshake or when they look at your business card. Your level of professionalism is suggested by your stationery, the way you follow up after an initial contact. The copy in your advertising and marketing

Every time you have a brief point of contact with a customer it speaks volumes about who you are and what you represent.

materials, the signs on your premises, the carpet and the décor. Your accessibility, the way you address your customer, the spelling of their name. All tiny little things. All important. All contribute to the message of who you are.

What message are you sending? Can you improve it?

Maximising the telephone as a Service instrument

The telephone is such a key instrument in today's business that it is nothing short of foolhardy to ignore its potential. And it doesn't take much. Sloppy telephone etiquette can cause no end of damage. For many companies, the telephone is the first point of call, which is why making it a good experience for the customer is so vital. Let's review the process.

It starts with the ring. In today's breakneck paced world, the perception of a wait-time continues to contract. Even four rings are too many. Many customers will hang up by the fifth ring. Those that don't are already on the wrong side of a good relationship. Two rings are considered the optimal, one ring and the customer is not ready herself, three rings and she is starting to wonder if anyone is there.

The greeting is simple and important. Something like this is acceptable: 'Good morning, ABC Company, this is Terry speaking.'

This is short enough not to bore your customer but has the essential salutation and other pertinent information.

This is short enough not to bore your customer but has the essential salutation and other pertinent information.

After your greeting, listen actively without interrupting, without judging; simply give full undivided attention.

If the customer is upset, acknowledge their emotions. Allow the emotions to run their course so that the customer feels listened to.

If the company has made a mistake, an admission is perfectly acceptable. Agree with your customer's right to complain.

This is all part of the rapport building process and adds to your empathy of your customer's situation.

Feed back your understanding of the information. Clarify the essence of the call and confirm that you have understood.

Offer to help and give choices. It is important for people to feel they have options. Options are inversely related to the level of customer's stress. Tell the customer what you will do. Then do it. Immediately.

Follow through with any promises you have made and report back to the customer. Remember the aim is to have the customer feel that you did everything in your power to rectify their complaint. The last but very important step is to thank them for bringing the matter to your attention. And mean it. Without their complaints, the business would be running blind.

The telephone is an exceptional Service tool – use it as such!

Action Steps

- Ask yourself, 'What kind of impression are we leaving with our customers? Are they thrilled, impressed or delighted or are they disappointed, confused and downright unhappy?'

- Explore the answers and then act in a way that leaves positive memories for every customer at every 'moment of truth'.

Remember the aim is to have the customer feel that you did everything in your power to rectify their complaint.

- Make some phone calls to your organisation, or get someone to do it on you behalf, and then assess the response. Could you do better?

- Make the most of every phone interaction with your customers.

CHAPTER FOURTEEN

Making A Difference

Badges of honour

People often wear price like a badge of honour. 'My dentist charges like a wounded bull… but damn, she's good', or, 'This tie cost me $380… but it sure makes me feel important'. Chances are you'd get the same dental treatment through a government-sponsored surgery and buy the same 'quality' tie for a tenth of the price. But that's not what counts. What counts is how these purchases make you feel.

How you make the customer feel is critical. If they feel they are getting preferential treatment, if they feel that they are buying quality, then that is what you are providing.

Chances are you'd get the same dental treatment through a government-sponsored surgery and buy the same 'quality' tie for a tenth of the price. But that's not what counts.

Parker Pens understand this. They don't sell pens; they sell the feeling that giving a great gift arouses. Hair salons don't sell haircuts; they sell you a good feeling while they give you counsel. Cosmetics companies don't sell cosmetics; they sell the feeling of hope.

When you serve customers, serve them a feeling and you won't have to worry about price.

177

Don't promise your customers value

Everybody promises value. Stop a thousand business people in the street and ask them what they provide for their customer. 'Value for money'. But value alone is a subjective thing. Alone it is invisible. What does value mean to your customer? Make it tangible. Unless you can make it 'real' you position yourself alongside everyone else. Saying you give value is meaningless, and while we are at it, so is giving a guarantee. Unless, and it is a big unless, you paint the picture very clearly of what this means for the customer.

Value alone is a subjective thing. Alone it is invisible.

Don't promise the customer value; promise them what value means to them.

Attention as a commodity

Ever increasing demands are made on our most precious resource – our attention. Advertisers vie for it at a rate of some 1,500 to 2,000 advertising messages a day. E-mail, fliers, posters, TV, radio, labels, T-shirts, websites, billboards and presentations all bombard us with their messages. Why, then, among all this advertising should your customer give you any attention? Only when you can show that your greatest interest is in them, will you have any chance of getting their attention. Everybody is chasing some of your customer's attention. The customer's attention is a rare commodity. As with any rare commodity, people part with it reluctantly, unless they can see that it is clearly in their best interests. If you want to be competitive when it comes to attention, focus on them.

Treat customers' attention as a rare and precious commodity.

Eavesdropping at the barbie

People focus on what is important to them. Picture this. You're at the end of year social barbie, engrossed in a conversation, when out of the blue someone mentions your name. Do you immediately tune into what they are saying? If you are like the rest of the world, the answer is yes. Why? Because our names are important to us and our brains are well adjusted to hear anything that is important to us. Your brain will automatically align with the greatest priority. Your customer's name is pretty high on her list. To get your customer's attention, use her name.

Everybody is chasing some of your customer's attention. The customer's attention is a rare commodity.

Personalise every conversation. Give your own name first and the customer will most likely reciprocate. Then use it early. There are plenty of courses available to help you learn people's names. Some are better than others. I recall a time that I was giving a seminar when someone came up to me in the break. 'Hi Terry,' they said and then proceeded to chat away as if I knew them like an old friend. I didn't. Rather than just being embarrassed, I simply apologised and asked where he knew me from. As it turns out, he'd been a participant in one of my previous seminars. In the course of any given year I meet thousands of people and so couldn't possibly be expected to remember all the names of people who attend my training programs. However, I did compliment him for remembering my name. He replied that it was easy since he had attended a course on remembering people's names. 'Great,' I replied enthusiastically, 'What was the name of the guy who ran the course?' He spent the rest of the time trying to remember. As I said, some courses are better than others. However, good courses on remembering names are a good investment.

'Great,' I replied enthusiastically, 'What was the name of the guy who ran the course?' He spent the rest of the time trying to remember.

Action Steps

- Send your people to courses that help them remember people's names.

- Encourage and reward your people for remembering customers by name.

- Develop strategies to get customers' names readily and without pressure.

- Get priority by personalising.

Don't try to be all things to all people

If, when you went fishing, you used every bait known to man and put it all on one line, chances are you'd catch very little. Except backache. For a start, it would probably sink to the bottom. If you try to please everybody with everything you run the same risk. Stay focused on what that customer wants, and deliver it in a way that gives the most impact. Under-promise and over-deliver. Concentrate on those customers to whom you can reliably deliver exceptional Service. If you try to provide a Service to the people that are obviously served better elsewhere, you will water down your Service and project an image of mediocrity. Work in the area where you can do really well and then work on making it even better. Only diversify where you know you can make a difference.

Making decisions takes time, so if you offer too many choices you'll confuse your customer.

Remember, you can't please all the people all the time, but you can serve some of the people exceptionally well.

Make it easy

Most customers like things easy. It's not because people are lazy, it is just that they have so little time. People today are resource-rich and time-poor. Therefore anything you do that makes it easy will stand you in good stead. This is true even of decisions. Making decisions takes time, so if you offer too many choices you'll confuse your customer. You are the adviser. You are the one with the expertise. If asked which colour, which size, what dimensions, have the answer. Make it easier for them by offering fewer choices. People don't appreciate being baffled with all the details.

Make it easy for your customer.

Emotive Language

Avoid emotive language. Certain phrases trigger angry responses. Most are in some way connected with the customer's perception that you are refusing to take responsibility for their concerns. Saying it is 'company policy' is an example. Customers think you are hiding behind this statement. And they are probably right. Recently my wife, Heather, went into the bank to deposit a cheque in the 'Fast service' facility. When she got there she noticed there were no deposit slips. Right next to the 'Fast service facility' a staff member was busying herself with one of those *'We give great service'* signs, so Heather asked her where the slips were. 'Oh, we don't leave them out,' she replied. 'You have to get them from the counter, that's new company policy'.

She was funny, genuine and took the time to banter with us like we were friends in a pub.

Being a fairly tolerant women, my wife waited in line. When she arrived at the counter she requested more than one deposit slip to save her queuing next time. 'Oh, we cant do that, we can only give you one slip at a time, that's (Yes, you guessed it) company policy'.

One solution is to have better *company policy*. Failing

182

that, though, it is wise to avoid these phrases altogether and in their place explain why the procedure is in place. For example, 'You'll want to give me your credit card details, sir, so I can get your (whatever it is they require) to you as soon as possible.'

Why our bank cant leave out the forms, however, remains a mystery to me.

Getting more than just a meal

Recently I took one of my clients for a meal. A sort of a thank you for being such a terrific client. It wasn't a particularly fancy restaurant. That didn't matter much because we received exceptional Service from the waitress. She was funny, genuine and took the time to banter with us like we were friends in a pub. And isn't that part of it? That ability to just have fun with people? I think that is an enormous part of excellent Service. Genuinely

You can never do enough for a terrific client.

enjoying other people and letting them enjoy you. The more you do this, the better the transaction. And in the final analysis, it will not only be more profitable, but it will be a better world as well.

Take every opportunity to make it a better world.

A special client

Christmas was approaching and the goose was getting fat. Has anyone ever stopped to think why the goose was getting fat? I don't know, but I do know that as

Christmas approached I was getting fat. Fat, with more money in my pocket, largely from the great relationship I had built with one very large organisation. This company alone had been worth tens of thousands of dollars to me in the last few months. My colleague and I had already taken out the key player to lunch, bought him drinks and said many thankyous. When I said to my friend that I was going to buy some of the key player's staff a drink as well, he responded that he thought we had done enough already. My reply? 'You can never do enough for a terrific client.'

These people become more than just clients. They become advocates, and sometimes even your friends.

And it is true. Key people not only bring in revenue directly, but if you foster the relationship, they can become your best source of referral. Key people can become a centre of influence that generates a whole raft of good opportunities for you. These people become more than just clients. They become advocates, and sometimes even your friends.

And it all begins with you treating them like special people – because they are. All people are special. It is our job to see what is special about them, and then focus on that.

Whenever possible, do something a bit special.

You can never say thank you too many times

It is said that repetition is the mother of skill. If that is true then it can also be said that the mother who is repetitious is skilful. I remember my mother must have told me she loved me at least 5 times every day, and because of that, I knew she did. Repetition is power.

When you are dealing with a customer always remember to tell them that you are grateful for their business. Now I don't mean that you have to tell them that you love them over and over again. In fact, I doubt you want to tell them you love them at all. But you do need to find ways

Customers hate entering a place of business and not being acknowledged.

that show them that you do care about them. People don't care how much you know, until they know how much you care.

Find ways to say thank you and then say it again, and again...

Poor Service is an opportunity

Numerous studies have been conducted to find out the things that most annoy customers. These studies affirm and support the informal feedback I have conducted with my clients. The top ten in no particular order are:

Ignorance: It's annoying if the person is ignorant about their Service. What bothers customers more is being treated as though they are ignorant.

Arrogance: This complaint is really an extension of the first one. Only this time the Service provider is more focused on themselves. They have filled themselves with a self-importance not befitting their role.

Being ignored: Customers hate entering a place of business and not being acknowledged. This doesn't mean they want to be pestered, but they do want to know that you are aware of their presence, and will provide assistance if required.

Being treated like an interruption: Have you ever been somewhere and the staff member is giving you that look that says and-what-is-it-that-you-want-can't-you-see-that-I-am-busy? Where they are giving audible tuts at the thought of having to break off whatever they're doing?

Stupidity: The kind of behaviour that just gets up your nose. People exhibiting such stupidity leave you shaking your head in disbelief.

Waiting: Making customers wait sends the message that their time is, at best, not as important as yours, and, at worst, not important at all.

Even so, when promised something, people are disappointed when it doesn't happen.

False appointment times: Doctor's surgeries are notorious for this. When you give customers a time to see you, they expect that you will actually see them at this time. If you are unable to make this time, let them know as soon as possible.

Hard sell: Customers get annoyed when they feel coerced into buying something. Even if it is something that they want, like and are ready to buy.

186

Rudeness: Customers expect to be treated with dignity and respect.

No follow through: This one is particularly annoying. In a world of suspicion where we are continually exposed to broken promises from politicians, advertisements that don't live up to their claims and even friends who don't keep their commitments, we have good reason to be distrustful. Even so, when promised something, people are disappointed when it doesn't happen.

Opportunities are everywhere

All these things are an opportunity to make our Service stand out from the crowd. Let's analyse them one by one.

Ignorance: There is sometimes a fine line between helping people make an informed decision and treating them as if they know nothing. It is a line we must walk. The only way to establish what advice the customer wants is to ask and listen. Careful listening will reveal the customer's knowledge. If they come into an IT shop talking of bits, processor speeds and CPUs, it is a fair bet that they want different advice from the person asking what size telly they get and where's the ON switch.

Arrogance: Customers are suspicious of providers who big-note themselves – and rightly so. And if the arrogance continues they not only suspect, they get darn right miffed. Meet the person at their level. They don't

187

care that you have a degree in metaphysical biology unless it is relevant to their immediate needs.

Being ignored: Most people don't like being ignored, so why should your customers? They don't. This doesn't mean they want to be pestered, because they don't want that either. But when they want Service, they want to know you will be there to serve them. Many years ago my wife, Heather, did training for hotel management. As part of that training, she had to learn to wait on tables. The waitresses were trained to be always watching what the patrons were doing while not being seen to be watching. A fine line. People providing a Service should tread this same fine line. Always ready when that customer wants something, and up to that point being distant enough not to seem intrusive.

Right at that moment they are our most important priority. Anything less could fairly be construed as poor Service.

Treated like an interruption: When a customer walks into your place of business or calls in on the phone, remember that they are the reason we exist. So they should have our undivided attention, making it clear to them that right at that moment they are our most important priority. Anything less could fairly be construed as poor Service. Phone calls can wait, arrangements for the weekend can wait and so can the filing or tidying of the paper-work. Always remember that the customer puts the bread on the table.

Stupidity: Being in business presumes that we know our business. If we don't know our own business well then we shouldn't be in business. The product knowledge, the expertise or whatever is needed in your line of business is crucial to providing quality Service. If we want to help the customer make an informed choice – and we do – then we'd best be informed ourselves. This goes for everyone handling the customer. Sometimes the staff member may not have all the knowledge, and in that case, they should know to whom the customer can speak to get the knowledge. There is no excuse for stupidity when it comes to Service.

Waiting: During the last holiday season I had the misfortune to be caught in the Christmas rush. Finding myself in a rather long queue, I decided to amuse myself by watching the other customers. And it was amusing. It is amazing how disgruntled people get when waiting in queues with nothing to do. There is a solution to this problem. Research has shown that customers are a lot more tolerant of standing in a queue if there is something to do. I found this true for myself. When I was a child, my parents took me to Disney Land – a Service Mecca. Although they had queues there, I never had a chance to be bored. They did a couple of things we can all learn from. Firstly, they gave better than accurate estimates on how long you would be waiting. How? By over-estimating your wait time. The queue moved faster that I expected. An example of under-promise and over-deliver. If you don't want to wait you can make an informed choice. And secondly they entertained those who chose to wait. With

If we want to help the customer make an informed choice – and we do – then we'd best be informed ourselves.

musicians, puppets and shows to keep the children and adults enthralled.

What can you do for your customers while they wait for your Service?

False appointment times: Whenever possible make appointment times that allow you enough of a buffer to accommodate any hiccups. If for any reason your schedule blows out, be sure to let them know. A simple thing, rarely done, but incredibly important as far as Service goes.

Hard sell: When people are pushed they push back, and hard selling is being pushed. It is not that customers do not like to be guided, advised and informed; they like all these things. But if for one moment they suspect that something is being rammed down their throats, the game is lost. Customers are more aware today, and know their rights. With cooling-off periods, statutory laws and other safeguards in place it is nothing short of foolhardy to press a sale upon a customer. The customer is the most important element in the equation of business success, so keep their best interests in mind. They require assistance, not coercion.

If for one moment they suspect that something is being rammed down their throats, the game is lost.

Rudeness: Rudeness can show itself in many ways, from the way a customer is spoken to, the way they are treated and the Service provider's actions. None are excusable. Simple pleases and thankyous go a long way to creating rapport with customers. Simple gestures, such as holding a door open and letting customers walk through first, leave lasting impressions. It takes so little to make a good impression, and importantly it takes so little to leave a bad one.

No follow through: Of all the annoyances that customers experience this is one of the easiest to correct and one that can have the greatest impact. Now people almost expect to get let down. You ask a friend if they can make it to your barbie on the weekend and they reply, 'I'll see if I can'. You know right there and then that they won't be there. The plumber says, 'I'll see if I can make it to your call-out before lunch time'. You don't even expect to see them before teatime at the earliest. This is just the way the world is, you tell yourself. Well, it doesn't have to be. If you want your organisation to be exceptional and stand out, the simplest – and one of the most powerful – things you can do is to make promises that you can and will keep.

The simplest – and one of the most powerful – things you can do is to make promises that you can and will keep.

Action Steps

- How many of these customer complaints are you guilty of? What can you do right now to make sure they don't happen in the future?

191

- Knowledge about these complaints should be music to your ear, because these are good opportunities for you to make your business exceptional.

- Let the poor Service of others be your opportunity for great Service.

CHAPTER FIFTEEN

Excellence Will Be Tolerated

The mischievous memory

The influence we get from others can sometimes be so powerful that it distorts reality. Until very recently I always thought that I was an exceptional student in my early school years. At least that was how I remembered it. I recall my Mum always saying to me, 'Son, you are so bright you could do or be anything you want.' I believed her. And in fact, the second part of her refrain was true. Upon the foundation of those words I have always done and been anything I chose.

The freedom to choose and then exercise that right has been my greatest asset. Because of those words, my memory of my performance at school was very positive. Then I found my old school reports. That shattered that belief. Oh, I was exceptional all right. Exceptionally dumb! Almost every report lamented over my poor ability. It is a good job Mum hid those reports for all those years otherwise I doubt I would have attempted and successfully accomplished even a quarter of the things I have achieved. Memory is

> *Oh, I was exceptional all right. Exceptionally dumb!*

a fickle animal, which can be easily tricked, and I now turn that to my advantage. You can too. When talking about your business, focus on the achievements and let failures of the past slip into obscurity.

In George Orwell's seminal novel, *1984*, knowledge is manipulable. The ruling regime – Big Brother – decreases chocolate rations from sixteen squares to twelve squares. After a short while the regime changes the ration to fourteen squares and celebrates the 'increase'. Big Brother recognised that people's most recent memory is the strongest. Customers, too, remember what you did last.

Action Step

- Make sure the last thing you do for your customers is positive.

- Use memory to advantage; focus on the wins.

Persevere in the face of doubt

'Don't throw the baby out with the bath water'. A well worn expression, but like many adages it is based on a truism. Sometimes we try something new to satisfy our customers, only to find that they remain equally dissatisfied. A leading bank in the U.S. surveyed their customers – there's another one of those damned surveys – to find out their pet peeves. The feedback stated that 'waiting in line' rated number one on the annoyance factor. 'Ah,' thought the higher echelons of the bank hierarchy, 'we are on a winner here. All we need to do is whack 'em through quicker and we'll be laughing all the way to the bank.' The bank then implemented a very expensive and labour-intensive strategy. A plan that reduced average waiting time down from just under five minutes to just over four minutes. A reduction of about half a minute. An exercise costing millions of American dollars. The end result? Customers were just as miffed as before.

Out went the surveys again. This time the customers identified their number one aggravation as... yeah, you guessed it... waiting in line. Most customers were not even aware that they were waiting a shorter

All we need to do is whack 'em through quicker and we'll be laughing all the way to the bank.'

time. The bank abandoned the idea and left the customers to deal with their frustration.

The idea was sound, only the approach could have been better. If the bank had actually spoken to their customers, they would have found out what really bothers people; that their time is being wasted. People are impatient. But they are only impatient if they feel their time is being wasted. This begs the question, 'How can you make sure that your customers *feel* that their time is not be wasted?' The answer: give them something of value while they are waiting. When a dentist by the name of Paddy Lund understood and implemented this idea, his business profits went up tenfold.

How does he do it? If you are lucky enough to be one of Paddy's patients – yes, lucky enough – you don't just go to an appointment and wait to be seen. You get there early to be entertained! His surgery is more like the lobby of a hotel where a quartet plays to you while you are served drinks. By the way, if you want to get an appointment with Paddy, you can't. Well, not unless you are referred by one of his existing clients. All of Paddy's work now comes from his referral base. In fact, he has made it a condition of doing business with him. All new patients agree to refer two people 'of equally high calibre' before they are seen. Oh, one other thing. Paddy is not cheap. But he gives excellent Service.

Action Steps

- Just because an idea doesn't work in its initial form doesn't mean it is a bad idea. Throw ideas around and try them on a small basis. If they don't work in that form, change them and try again.

- Think outside the box. Look at what other industries do.

Beware strong convictions

'Everyone is thinking what I am thinking.' Ever had this thought? Big mistake. Every

If you want to get an appointment with Paddy, you can't.

thought is as unique as the person thinking it. Sure, you could be thinking along the same lines. But then again, you may not be. When you get caught up in 'status-quo' thinking, it is sometimes difficult to break free. Fortunately, the signs of such thinking are easy to spot. When your people start saying things like,

'We all reckon the customers see it that way' or, 'Everyone agrees that giving customers a 24 hour turn-around time is ridiculous', alarm bells should ring. This kind of talk is not just an over generalisation; it can be downright dangerous.

Some people are very good at convincing others that their view is the only view. Which of course it isn't. I recall running a program for a large organisation which illustrated this point clearly. My colleague and I were brought into the organisation when things were, shall we say, a bit bleak. Consequently, the staff were suspicious of the management's motives.

'Why are you here? Have you been brought in to soften the blow? Are we being out-sourced?' These were just some of the typical comments. From the first day, we knew we had our work cut out for us. After an extensive program, there had been a marked turnaround in attitude. The group re-evaluated their reason for being there and their attitude towards

People are impatient. But they are only impatient if they feel their time is being wasted.

Service within the organisation. However, one participant, while agreeing that the course was worthwhile, remained unchanged in his attitude toward management. He expressed it this way. 'We have gotten good results from this course, but everyone here still thinks that the management is trying to out-source us.'

I said, 'Everyone? Let's put it to the test.'

Not one other person agreed with him. Left

unchecked, such negative thinking can influence others and stifle any positive expectations of the organisation and the customers.

Action Steps

- Always check what people are thinking. And you can't know what people are thinking until you ask them. In more ways than one.

- Find ways to make it easy for people to give candid feedback at all times. Create a Culture of open communication.

- Question dogmatic belief systems.

Perfection and procrastination: twin cousins

'Perfection is our goal, but excellence will be tolerated.' I once worked with an organisation where the chairman had these words emblazoned upon a plaque on his desk. At first glance, this seemed a worthwhile attitude to take. After working with him for a while I realised that we needed to qualify this statement. People need to know that it's okay to do something badly first, and then strive for higher things.

Sometimes excellence, and even perfection, is possible in the mind of the customer. But not always.

This particular chairman didn't hold this view, which turned out to be counter-productive. His staff were often hamstrung for fear of not reaching his level of excellence. Instead of doing something to the best of their ability, they were paralysed and did nothing. They found it easier to make excuses than to live up to such unreasonable expectations.

This is not to suggest that you shouldn't have high expectations for your people. You should. Rather, I am saying set the bar at a level that affords them a stretch, not an impossible task. Sometimes excellence, and even perfection, is possible in the mind of the customer.

Being off-course was simply a necessary part of the journey.

But not always. A consistently high standard, with moments of excellence and perfection, is a far more achievable goal. High performance is a more sustainable norm.

Move away from perfection to performance.

Action Step

- Encourage people to do their best when their best is what you require. People need to know it is all right to have a go, even if they fall short of excellence.

Failure is feedback

Most things in life are off-course much of the time. At age nineteen I earned my private pilot's licence. This taught me many things. Not just flying. I learned that the phrase 'as the crow flies' does not mean in a straight line. Neither crows nor planes fly in a perfectly straight line. Although I plotted courses to given destinations in straight lines, that was not an indication of how the aircraft flew. My job as the pilot was to monitor the gauges and the lie of the land to keep pulling the plane back on track. Because for ninety percent of the time it wasn't. Did the fact that I could not keep my aircraft on course make me a failed pilot? Of course not, because being off-course was just feedback. As long as I was clear about my final destination. My goal. Then, being off-course was simply a necessary part of the journey. So it is with your Service delivery. When you are making changes to the way you implement Service, expect hiccups along the way. Because you are going to get them. Treat them as feedback and a way to fine-tune your Service.

Action Step

- Treat mistakes, slip-ups and errors as small deviations from the bigger goal. Encourage others to treat them as trifles and minor setbacks along the road to excellence.

Feedback is fine-tuning, not failure.

The glory of goals

The power of goals only became apparent to me by accident. After graduating from university, I was unsure of a career choice. So, instead of entering the work force I decided to research the notion of success. I began devouring success literature furiously. The common denominator I found in all writings around success – company, country or individual – was the need to set clear directional goals. I set about getting my first personal goal in writing. I began by creating my ideal job in my mind and on paper. I set up some fairly stringent criteria for my career. I wanted to be within cycling distance of my home. I wanted to be the manager of an office – never having done this before. I wanted incredible autonomy. I wanted my own personal secretary. I wanted a view from my office window. And so the list went on!

It was no more than twelve months when I not only achieved my goal as written, but exceeded all expectations. I was a believer. I have since spent thousands of hours either teaching or researching the thoughts and words of great goal setters. I can sum it up in just two. It works!

Goals need to be specific – you can't hit a target unless you know what the target looks like.

What I have found out is that if goals are to work to their full potential then they need to be set in a specific way. Not exactly the same way, but at least with the following elements.

Goals need to be specific – you can't hit a target unless you know what the target looks like. Include an element of measurability in the goal setting process. For some goals that is really easy, such as meeting a financial goal or a sales performance goal. For some goals, it is more difficult. However, a measure of time is always possible.

Giving a goal a time-frame creates a sense of urgency.

The goal must be feasible. Remember that most things are feasible for someone. So, be careful not to restrain yourself here.

You must fervently believe that you can reach your goal. This is probably the greatest deciding factor in any goal setting process.

And finally the goal must be committed to paper. Look at the written goal often and it serves as a constant reminder to you and your commitment. Nothing real new here, these ideas are timeless truths. I include them because any program on achieving change for the better would be an impoverished work without goals. Creating a culture of Service Excellence requires change. It therefore requires goals.

Set goals – they work!

Action Step

- Set goals that follow a winning formula. The one that has worked for me and countless others includes the ideas outlined above.

Great Service isn't an accident

McDonalds didn't become the leader in family dining through a windfall. B-Digital didn't grow from eight to three hundred by chance. Luck wasn't the deciding factor in Honda's phenomenal success. They all had something in common: A plan spawned from a dream. Sound planning underpins any successful business. And more specifically, a plan of how to best Serve their customers. The key to their planning was to think beyond externally imposed boundaries, refusing to limit themselves to constraints within their industry.

This is not always easy to do, as some prominent people have discovered only in hindsight. Even leaders in a field, immersed in their business, can still miss the mark. The computer industry has some interesting examples of predictions. Tom Watson, founder of IBM is quoted as saying, 'I think there is only a world market for maybe five computers.' And who could forget Bill Gates' quote, 'Two hundred and

The key to their planning was to think beyond externally imposed boundaries, refusing to limit themselves to constraints within their industry.

fifty kilobytes should be enough for anyone.' Great business leaders may not have a crystal ball, but as the mist clears, they are certainly the first to take advantage of any glimmer of opportunity. Out of the mists dreams are born.

Ray Kroc of McDonalds dreamed of a network of restaurants stretching across the USA. The founders of B-Digital envisioned accessible mobile phones, and Honda dreamed of a world full of cost-effective transport. First they dreamed and then they planned.

Dream, plan and then realise! A Culture of Service Excellence awaits you.

Action Steps

- Begin dreaming of a better world. Proclaim the dream a goal. Chart a course and move assuredly toward your chosen destination.

- Encourage others to dream, ponder and wonder about a better world. Listen to their ideas. Encourage their ideas and nurture their dreams.

CONCLUDING COMMENTS

What is Success?

I began this book with a poem from Ralph Waldo Emerson. For more than two hundred years, now, the words of Emerson have inspired, motivated and empowered individuals and corporations to create a better world. A world where intangible things matter; the invisible things of love, caring and the feelings of people. A world where Service to others is held as the highest good. Throughout his work and his life Emerson knew, lived and wrote about the virtues of Service Excellence. Of all the words he wrote, however, none sum it up more succinctly and so eloquently as the last stanza in his famous poem – What is Success? A stanza that is the essence of Focusing on The Invisible and creating a Culture of Service Excellence. I leave you with his words. I wish you success:

To know that even one life has breathed easier because you have lived;

This is to have succeeded.

VISION
IS THE ABILITY
TO SEE
THE INVISIBLE

Jonathan Swift

Contacting the Author

I would love to hear from you to discuss *'Focusing on The Invisible'* in your organisation, or any of the ideas in this book. I can be contacted at:

Tel: 0419 148 418
+61 8 9537 3889
Email: terry@execedge.com.au
Website: www.execedge.com.au

About the Author

Terry delivers keynote presentations, interactive conferences, team events and consultancy to help you Focus on the Invisible and Create a Culture of Service Excellence. He has worked with corporations, educational institutions, community organisations and the public sector. Terry also works to create other aspects of personal and corporate development. See his Web site for more information: www.execedge.com.au

ADDITIONAL COPIES OF
"FOCUSING ON THE INVISIBLE"
ARE AVAILABLE FROM:

Comet Publishing
18 Bight Reefs Road
Singleton 6175
Western Australia

Phone: 0419 148 418
Fax: +61 8 9537 3889
Email: comet@execedge.com.au